FROM A STREET KID

Stephen Lungu's Incredible Life-journey

COSMOS PRESS

From A Street Kid
Copyright © Tonia Cope Bowley 2024

www.toniacopebowley.co.uk

The moral right of the author has been asserted.

All rights reserved

No part of this publication may be reproduced, stored in a retrieval system, or transmitted in any form or by any means, without the prior permission in writing of the publisher, nor be otherwise circulated in any form of binding or cover other than that in which it is published.

First published in Great Britain 2012
Second Edition 2024

ISBN paperback: 978-0-9935332-4-2
ISBN eBook: 978-0-9935332-5-9

eBook design by IngramSpark
Illustrations by Niko Petropouleas
Cover illustration by Louis de Jager

A catalogue record of this book is available from the British Library

*In memory of, and in gratitude
for the extraordinary life of
Stephen Lungu
1942 – 2021*

Tell this to your children,
and let your children tell it to their children,
and their children, to the next generation.
Joel 1:3

Inside

PART 1 REJECTED	1
PART 2 A CHICKEN RUN	15
PART 3 ON THE STREETS	25
PART 4 TURBULENT TIMES	35
PART 5 GANG LIFE	47
PART 6 TURNING POINT	67
PART 7 SURRENDER	85
PART 8 VALUED	95
PART 9 SHOCKS AND SURPRISES	105
PART 10 TOUGH TRAINING	119
PART 11 LOVE AND MARRIAGE	129
PART 12 DEALING WITH THE PAST	145
PART 13 TOP JOB	165
STEPHEN'S MESSAGE FOR YOU	177
THANK YOU	179
IN GRATITUDE	180
LAST WORDS	181
ABOUT THE AUTHOR	182

Part 1
REJECTED

1 Stephen arrives

A new pair of lungs bellowed out Stephen's arrival on this planet. A few minutes later the noise-level reduced to a whimper as he was placed in his Mama's arms. For a long time Elenita stared at him in silence in a jumble of awe and growing panic.

Elenita's young life tumbled before her eyes. So many whys? Why, when she was just thirteen, had her parents arranged her marriage against her will? Why had they chosen someone so old and who had had other wives? Why was he so demanding and difficult? Why, whenever she ran away from him had her parents always sent her back? Why at fourteen, when she felt like a child and wanted to be looked after, had she become a mother? Would she survive?

Stephen's Mama felt so alone. She did not want to be married. She did not want a baby – at least not then. Yet, seeing her good-looking firstborn son, she realised none of her problems were his fault. She would muddle through.

At least Elenita liked their little home in Highfield, a quiet part on the outskirts of the city of Salisbury, Rhodesia in Southern Africa. Today it is called Harare in Zimbabwe. It was where Elenita had lived since she was a child and her family were all still there.

2   Early years with Mama

In the beginning life was mostly good for Stephen. He spent time alone with his Mama cuddling, feeding, and sleeping. Whenever he woke she was near.

When he was about two his brother John was born. Things changed. He had to share his mother's attention just when he became sickly and needed her most. He coughed a lot and his chest was sore. Mama moaned to her sisters about him and got snappy with Stephen. She would say:

> "Ah Stephen, why are you always sick? What shall I do with you? I have no money. I can't take you to hospital until Papa comes home. Where *is* your Papa? He's been gone a long time."

Mama was unhappy. For comfort she would reach under the bed for her hidden jug of beer and drink from it deeply. This frightened Stephen as it caused her to become violent.

Sometimes Mama would stretch out on her bed with Stephen and John next to her, stroke their heads and talk quietly to them. This made Stephen happy.

As he lay there he listened to the chickens cluck-clucking and scratching in the dirt

outside in the warm sunshine.

3   Papa

Stephen's Papa was short, trim and fit. At nearly fifty he married Elenita. She was only thirteen.

Papa's friends called him Chiwaya which means 'Big Gun' in English, maybe because he had fought in the First World War. He could be hard and cruel and would stay away without telling his wife where he was going or how long he would be gone. When he came home he wanted her to look after his every wish.

Stephen liked Sundays. On Sundays Papa was different. He shaved, washed his hair and looked smart. On their walk to church he smiled at people and said good morning. He was a leader and a popular preacher. He spoke in angry bursts, like thunder thought Stephen. He knew how to make people feel guilty. They nodded when they agreed with him.

Chiwaya was not Papa's real name. It was William Tsoka. Tsoka means 'unlucky', a name that suited him. Papa worked as a telephone repair man for the government in Salisbury. One day his boss told him that he would have to move to a new job in Bindura, a town 80 kilometers away. Elenita tried to stop the move but that resulted in horrible arguments. So, the day came when they packed up their little home and moved. They knew no one in Bindura.

4 Big move, big shock

They were all miserable in Bindura. Papa worked and was constantly in a bad mood. John screamed all night. Stephen wished they had never left Highfield. To try to escape her loneliness Mama drank more and more beer. She was always tired and Stephen noticed she was growing fat.

Papa seemed to hate Mama and spoke horridly to her. One night Stephen overheard him say:
"Stephen is not my son. He doesn't look like me."
"He *is* your child," sobbed Mama.
Papa did not believe her and kept going on:
"No, he is not."
"Who is my father?" Stephen asked himself.
For days he could think of nothing else. His world was falling apart.

One night Papa was especially angry. Like a roaring raging lion he sprang at Mama and beat her up. Stephen rushed at Papa and grabbed his legs.
"Stop it!" he yelled.
Papa kicked him to the other side of the room and went on beating Mama until she screamed:
"I am going to kill myself."
Stephen did not know what 'kill' meant but by the sound of her voice he knew it must be something terrible. Papa stormed out. Mama sobbed for hours. Then John joined in.

5   Back to Highfield

Not long after that Mama got news from Highfield. One of her relatives had died. Immediately she said:
 "I am going home for the funeral, and the birth."
Papa glared but before he could speak she was packing. Stephen was excited.
 "Getting away from Papa will be quality.
 I will see auntie's chickens too."
But what Stephen did not know was what Mama meant by 'the birth'.

Mama struggled to the train station carrying John and their luggage. Stephen tried to keep up. It was a long hot journey to Salisbury and they had little to eat and drink. Stephen liked the train. He looked out of the window watching animals, trees and people. The sky seemed so big and the clouds racing so high up were always changing their shapes.

"Salisbury!" a man shouted as the train stopped. They grabbed their stuff and walked to Elenita's parents' home. It felt safe there. After some food they went to bed. Stephen dozed off feeling happier than he had for a long time. Papa was far away so there were no arguments.

But, after only a few weeks Papa turned up and they moved to their old home. The government had sent him back to his old job. Stephen kept out of Papa's way. Often, he quietly thought:
 'You say you are not my father. Who is?"

6 Blame

A lot was changing. Malesi was his new baby sister so Stephen knew what 'the birth' meant! Mama looked thinner. She was only nineteen and had three small children to feed and look after. Mama no longer had time to spend with Stephen. He still coughed a lot but she did not notice any more. She often asked him to take care of John who was then three. John was almost as big as Stephen and always up to mischief.

Papa spent most of his time somewhere else. When he was at home he shouted at Mama all the time and said things Stephen did not understand. Mama was always cross especially when Papa stayed away at night.

Then, out of the blue, the very worst thing happened. A terrifying thought arrived in Stephen's head:
 "I must be the cause of all their unhappiness.
 Papa does not love Mama because of *me*."
This horrified Stephen. He was miserable. Then he grew to hate himself.

7 Papa walks out

When Stephen was about seven, Papa disappeared for weeks at a time. Sometimes Mama cried all day. Her sisters visited and talked to her in wailing whispers. After a while Papa did not come home at all.

Mama told Stephen Papa had gone to work far away and left them behind. Stephen was shocked. How could he? How would they get money to live? Although Mama worked on the lands some days, with other women, the pay was not good.

Stephen kept on blaming himself.
"It must be *my* fault.
I must have done something wrong."
But he just didn't know what to do.

8   Mama vanishes

One unforgettable afternoon, sometime after Papa left, Stephen and John were playing in the dust near to their home. Suddenly Mama came out of the house holding a clean and neat Malesi.
"Stephen and John hurry!
We are going into town", she called.

It was a long time since Mama had taken them on an outing so they jumped up and raced to her, both demanding to hold her free hand. Stephen won! They had fun looking in the shop windows. Mama wasn't interested and hurried them along. When they came to the market place, Stephen tugged on her skirt and asked her to stop so he could watch a man unloading a lorry full of vegetables but she walked on even faster.

When they came to the Amato Shopping Centre she stopped. It was a big place. Stephen and John stared wide eyed at everything. They had never seen so many people. Mama seemed to be looking for something. Suddenly she turned and said sternly:

"Stephen, stay here."
"What?"

Stephen was terrified. He tried to tell her he did not want to stay there without her but his words didn't seem to reach her ears. She peeled his little fingers away from hers. Then, with fear in her voice, she said:

"I must go to the toilet."

Mama pushed Malesi into his arms. Stephen almost dropped his wriggling baby sister. With that she said:

"Look after her.
Don't let John run off.
Stay together."

Mama seemed upset and angry.
"Yes, Mama."

Mama placed her hands on his head for a moment then walked away quickly without looking back. She vanished into the crowd.

9 Terrified

Five-year-old Stephen was in charge. Mama had hardly gone out of sight when Malesi began to cry. John stamped in the dust playing some game.

Strangers stared. After what seemed forever, Malesi fell asleep.

For a while Stephen sat holding his baby sister. He scanned the Shopping Centre again and again and stared at the spot where he'd last seen his mother. But that was hours ago. Why was she taking so long?

Stephen was tired and hungry. His arms ached from carrying Malesi. He felt rooted to the ground by her weight. His eyes seldom left the door of the women's toilet as he looked out for his Mama. But she had vanished.

John stubbed his toe and yelled like a dog that had been kicked. Malesi woke and joined in. Stephen stopped trying to be brave and cried too. It was getting late. The sun had almost gone to bed. The deepening dark terrified Stephen. They were miserable. No mother. What could they do? Where could they go?

10   The hate-giant

Stephen felt so alone, abandoned, helpless and worthless. Utter despair visited him for the first time. Mama was never coming back. He could trust no one. Then, right out of the blue, a giant invaded Stephen's life – the hate-giant. The hate-giant quickly filled his mind to overflowing until there was no room for any other thought.

"Mama hates me. Papa disowns me. He hates me.
I must be the reason they fight all the time."

Stephen realised that more than hating anyone else he hated himself. The hate-giant was a monster. It filled him with bitterness. Never before had he felt more miserable. He had nowhere to go, nowhere to hide.

11   The police station

After a long time a grown up spoke to them.
   "Where is your mother?" she asked.
This brought on a fresh round of deafening yelling.
   "Mama I want my Mama."

Soon they were surrounded by people wanting to help. Then a policeman arrived. He tried to talk to them but all they did was cry and scream. After a bit he gave up asking questions and took them to the police station. At the desk the duty policeman looked worried. After a while he picked up Malesi but nearly dropped her. Looking down at his shirt he grumbled:
   "Smelly wet babies!"
Another policeman took screaming Malesi away.

Stephen and John sat on a bench holding hands.
   "What are your names? Who is your mother? Why are you not with her?"
John stuffed one grimy fist into his mouth. Big tears rolled down Stephen's cheeks as he managed to say:
   "She's gone. Gone and left us."

Then a lady came into the room and looked at Malesi.

"She's too young and not well.
She must go into hospital."
She turned to Stephen and John and said:
"Would you like to come to the orphanage?"
That was not what they wanted and they started crying again. They were taken there anyway.

12　The orphanage

Stephen and John were taken to a long room with lots of beds and put next to each other. They sobbed and sobbed and finally fell asleep.

In the morning the orphanage-people came to talk to them. They discovered that they came from Highfield Township and had aunts living there.
"Tell us the names of your aunts."
Stephen could only remember their first names but that seemed enough. Then they were taken outside to play. Stephen and John sat huddled together, hands over faces, peeping at the other children.

Out of nowhere, some big boys rushed at Stephen separating him from John. They beat him up then rushed off laughing leaving Stephen in a soggy heap. A teacher spotted him.
"Why are you crying?" he asked.
"Big boys beat me up," Stephen stammered.
"What are their names?"
"I don't know. I've only just arrived."

The teacher exploded:
"I'll teach you to mess me around, boy."
He grabbed Stephen, tied his hands to a pole, pulled his pants down and his shirt up, and lashed him twelve times. Stephen screamed. That night his back was so sore he could not sleep. But that was not the end. For the next three days that 'punishment' was repeated.

On the fourth day little boy Stephen told himself:
"I must be a man – be strong."
So, when the lashes landed he did not utter a word or cry. This enraged the teacher but Stephen stayed silent bottling up his pain, anger and resentment.

The next day Stephen and John noticed a large hat walking into the orphanage. Suddenly they saw who was under it - Aunt-M! They raced up to her arms outstretched but she was stiff as starch and ice cold. They clung tightly onto her skirts.
"Aunty," they cried out together.
They were so pleased see someone they knew. But Aunt-M just glared and shook them off vigorously.
"*Where* is your mother?
Why aren't you with her?
Why have they called *me* here?"

Aunt-M walked away and went to talk to the people in charge. She was there for ages. At last she came back looking as black as a moonless midnight.
"Good God! I have enough problems."

Then, with a shove, she sent the boys flying down the orphanage steps into the bright sunshine.

Part 2
A CHICKEN RUN

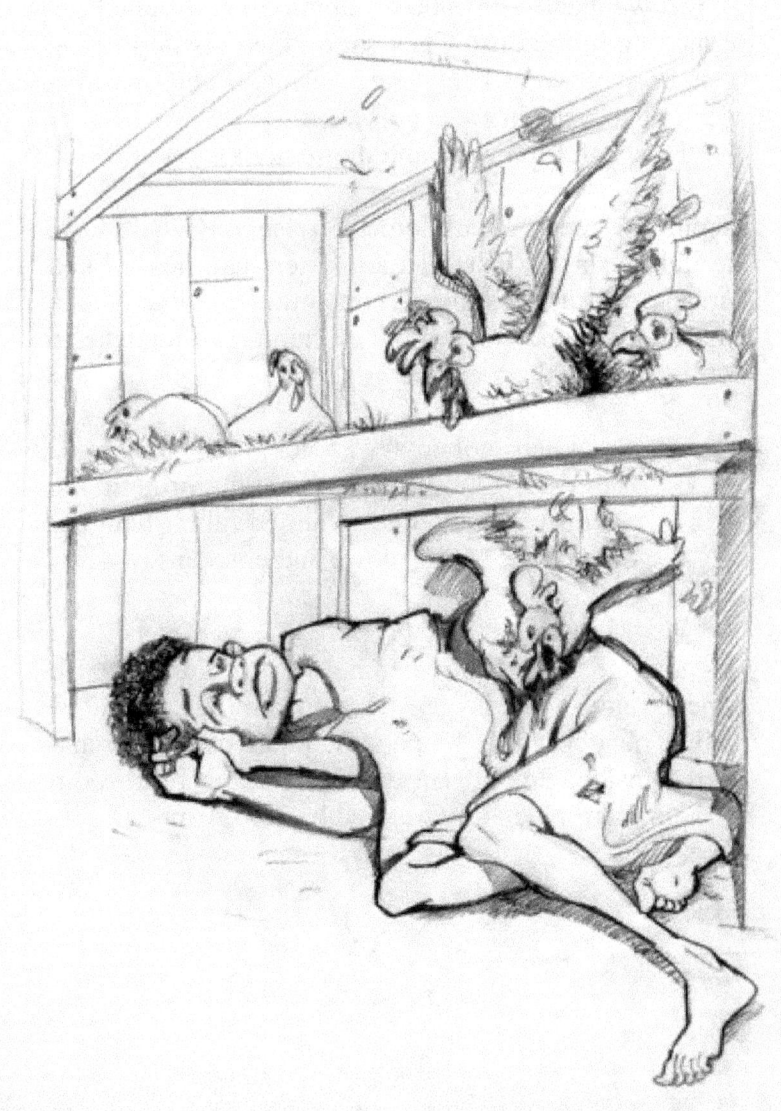

13   Living with Aunt-M

Stephen and John arrived at Aunt-M's small brick house. They were not happy. Their whole world seemed worse than ever before. Although only a short walk from their old home it felt like another country.

They wandered around watching the chickens scratching in the dust. They sat on the doorstep trying to hear what was being said inside. Everyone was speaking at once in cross voices:
 "How can Eletina go and dump her kids on us?"

Stephen wished he was someone else, anywhere else. He did not know that Mama's sisters had never liked her. She was always the odd one out. Now that Mama had run away they took it out on her kids. Stephen did not like any of them either.

When nobody was looking he slipped away. Out of sight he ran through the dusty streets like a hunted rabbit dodging people, trucks, cows and chickens.

His heart missed a beat when he saw his old home. He hoped Mama would open the door and all would be well. The door didn't open. Stephen pushed it and peered inside. Empty! He wandered about from room to room then reluctantly trudged back to Aunt-M's.

14 Uncaring aunts

Stephen and John were moved every few days between Aunt-M and her sisters. They were not welcome anywhere. They slept on floors with an old blanket for cover. They ate scraps from the table or what they found outside. They were often beaten.

Then, one after another, the aunts refused to look after them. Aunt-M did not want them either but felt obliged to have them. Stephen was always in trouble. Mostly it was not his fault. Aunt-M's lazy son discovered he could skip his tasks and blame Stephen. Aunt-M always believed her son.

15 Township school

January, the middle of summer in that part of Africa, was when the new school year began. To get Stephen out of her way, Aunt-M sent him to the township school. He was eight and in the first class but he didn't understand the teacher and so never did the work. He was miserable and even wet his pants.

Stephen could not see the point of school. He often bunked and fell further behind. At break times the other children played happily in the dust. Stephen wandered round the township looking longingly at kids with their parents. He asked himself:
"Why was I born into my crazy family?

Why am I not like other children?
They have two parents who want them."
Stephen was certain no one in the world loved him. He did not like himself and wished he would die.

16 Bullied

One sunny day Stephen was daydreaming as he walked around kicking stones when from nowhere a problem arrived. A gang of boys rushed out from behind the chicken run and surrounded him shouting:

"You have no parents.
You're so small!
We're going to get you."

Fists flew. Stephen screamed. John was not far away and ran to see what was going on. At six he was bigger and stronger than Stephen. When he saw the boys beating up his brother, he let out a roar and rushed into the middle of the gang kicking and fighting. They all fled. As Stephen picked himself up John said:

"If those bullies touch you again, tell them I'll beat them up good and proper."

The gang did bully Stephen again but, as he'd promised, John always sorted them out. John was Stephen's only supporter in a scary world.

17   Papa turns up

After what seemed like forever to Stephen, the year was over. In the holidays he and John spent their all time together. They invented games and talked to the chickens. They found lots to laugh about. All too soon the new school year started. Stephen was put into Class Two. He had not passed Class One and could not read or write.

One day without warning, Stephen's difficulties were solved, at least for a while. As he and John strolled towards home they heard a man's voice. It was Papa talking to Aunt-M. John got a huge hug. Stephen got a nod. The bottom dropped out of his world.

Aunt-M beamed as Malesi sat happily on her lap.
   "Your father's back and you can live with him."
The old rejected feeling flew to Stephen's stomach.
   "Come on you boys," Papa said suddenly.
   "Let's first go and buy some things."

With that they walked out of Aunt-M's house.

18   A far away country

Papa tricked Aunt-M. They did not go to the shops but hopped on a bus to the train station. When the train pulled in there was a mad scramble to find seats.

It was a long journey. Papa said they were going to Salima, in Malawi, north of Rhodesia. He was born there. Now that he was no longer working but had a pension, he was going back to his early home.

Papa had married again. His fourth wife (W-4) had her own children. She did not know Stephen and John were coming and they were not welcome. The home was not happy. Papa shouted at W-4 and beat her. She took it out on Stephen. John was bigger and stronger and was not afraid to fight back so he was left alone. After a while Papa moved them to his sister's home. More trouble! She expected a share of his pension but got nothing so again Stephen and John suffered.

19 Stephen's escape

Stephen often dreamt of going back to Highfield – but how? One day he was talking to some old ladies and told them of his dream. They understood.

"Poor Stephen, Papa doesn't want you. W-4 doesn't want you. Go back to Highfield."

"But I have no money," Stephen said miserably.

"You have a bicycle.

You could sell that to pay for your ticket!"

The old ladies explained how to get to the railway station and where he should change trains.

Stephen sold his bicycle and in a few days he was off.

20 Stowaway

The station was busy with trains coming and going. No one noticed Stephen creep onto the platform. The old ladies had told him that to get to Salisbury he should first take a train to Blantyre.

Shaking from head-to-toe Stephen moved towards the train. He had no ticket. His bicycle money was everything he owned so he had decided to keep it. Train doors opened noisily. He squeezed his small body into a dark space next to a pile of crates.

The next day the scorching sun streamed down from a cloudless African sky as the train snaked its way through villages and countryside. Stephen was parched and hungry.

When the train stopped he hopped off and headed for the water tank. Then his luck turned. A motherly woman invited him to sit with her family and share their delicious food. Whenever they heard the ticket man coming they hid Stephen under their long skirts!

Eventually they reached Salisbury. Doors banged opened and people spilled out. Luggage and porters were everywhere. Chaos! Stephen had no problem leaving the train unnoticed.

21 Not you!

"It's cool to be back," thought Stephen as he dodged tall white people with their black porters.

At ten years old, Stephen was expert at dodging fares. He hopped on a bus heading for Highfield, and off at the right stop, avoiding the ticket man. People, stray dogs, cows and the odd chicken wandered about.

As he rounded the corner to Aunt-M's house he heard voices. He watched the smoke from the cooking fire as it curled upwards into the darkening sky. Aunt-M emerged holding her cooking pot. She poked the fire before she noticed the small boy standing staring at her. When he didn't go away she looked harder.
"Not *you*!
She screamed as she staggered to her feet and strode down the path. She caught Stephen by the ear.
"What in God's name are you doing here?
Stephen gulped.
"I did not like it in Salima so I came home."
"*Home*!" she yelled. "*This* is not your home."

Aunt-M jerked Stephen by his tatty top and in her rage held him with one hand and slapped and punched him with the other. She threw him to the ground and kicked him.

"What cheek you have coming back to me."

22 Chicken run

Stephen wished he'd never left Malawi. Aunt-M dragged him screaming into the chicken run.
"Don't think you will stay in my house."
The chickens were flustered. Stephen sobbed until he could sob no more. His teeth chattered from shock and the rapidly cooling African night.

He spotted an old dirty sack, lay down and pulled it over him. He was thinking of the warm train and the mama who had been kind to him. Aunt-M appeared and pushed some scraps through the chicken wire. He gobbled these up.

The next day Aunt-M let Stephen out.
He felt pain in her presence. She did not want him. He did not want to be there but he could not return to Malawi. They were kind of stuck with each other – at least for a while.

Days and nights went by. Sometimes Stephen slept on the floor in the house under a tatty blanket. But when Aunt-M was in a bad mood he slept with the chickens.

To pay Aunt-M for letting him stay Stephen did odd jobs like sweeping the house, cleaning the chicken run, fetching water, and anything else she wanted him to do. Once the jobs were done, she didn't want Stephen around and told him to 'clear off'. He was happy to get out of her sight and left quickly in case he got called back to do another job.

Part 3
ON THE STREETS

23   Dustbin take-aways

Stephen was eleven, skinny as a stick, and always famished. He left the house that day desperate to find food. Soon he stopped at the edge of a group of men sitting beside the road, laughing and drinking beer. A man was pointing at his shoes.
   "Tell us where you got them," someone said.
   "My boss threw them in the garbage bin.
   Whites even throw out clothes and food."
At the mention of food Stephen nearly fell over.

Swiftly he slipped away unnoticed. As he walked to the edge of the Big City he was afraid. He had never been into a white area but his hunger was stronger than his fear. Worn out he arrived at a wide shady road between big gardens belonging to fine bungalows. Large dogs scared him. He walked on quietly until he spotted a service road at the back of the houses where the garbage bins were kept. With eyes like saucers he moved towards the nearest bin.
   "What will I find – a feast?

Slowly Stephen lifted the lid. The stink of rotting food made him feel sick. He banged the lid back on and backed off. Hunger drove him back. Armed with a stick he sifted through moldy oranges and slimy stuff. A blob of porridge mixed with decaying vegetables surfaced. He scooped up a mouth full and swallowed the disgusting stuff. Then he rushed into the bushes and was as sick as a dog.
   "Mama, why did you leave me?" he sobbed.
   "Where are you?"
But no Mama came to cuddle and comfort him.

Stephen explored the bins again. That time he found dry burnt toast and a half a mango decorated with tea leaves. Then yummy! He found a meaty bone.

It was dangerous to be found in a white area after dark so when the sun was getting low he turned homewards. Aunt-M was in a bad mood and put him in the chicken run. But, for the first time since his meal on the train, he did not feel hungry and slept soundly.

24 Unexpected company

Stephen was no longer at school so had lots of spare time. Visiting the garbage bins was routine. He became expert on where to find the best take-aways. No one bothered him.

There came a day when Stephen wasn't alone. He'd noticed a bin with the lid half off and went to inspect. As he carefully lifted the lid and peered inside a pair of bright eyes looked up at him, whiskers twitching. A huge, fierce rat was grazing on the sticky mess inside.

"Ugh! You revolting rat!" Stephen screamed as the mammoth rat leapt out of the bin, brushing past him.

He never got used to the disgusting smell of garbage.

25 The golf club

Dreaming about his future Stephen thought he wanted to be a servant in a white home wearing squeaky clean white clothes. The problem was, he thought:
"I am not designed for such a posh life!"

As Stephen pressed his nose against the fence of the nearby golf club, he thought he'd like to be a caddy. He watched the older black teens carrying the white men's golf clubs. After some months they allowed him to sit with them while they waited for a caddy-job. One day a tall white man asked Stephen to caddy.
"Yes, sir," he said eagerly.

The man pointed to his clubs and started walking. Stephen grabbed the bag handle and heaved. Nothing moved no matter how hard he tried. He was so frustrated he almost cried. But instead of being told off the man said gently:
"I'm so sorry. I put too many clubs in my bag.
But you tried, so here, you can have my small change."

Stephen stared at him. He'd never known such kindness and it was the first time a white man had spoken to him.

26 Money grabber

The boys let Stephen into a secret.
"Go to the tennis club.
You could earn money collecting balls."
Stephen hurried. He got a job and found it easy. By the time he was twelve he was an expert ball boy. The club was like his home. He belonged. He was happy, had friends, and fun.

Stephen saved until he had enough money to buy a new shirt as his was falling to bits. Feeling smart he walked back to Aunt-M's. With a look of horror she grabbed him, shook him and demanded to know where he'd got money for the shirt. When she realised he was working at the tennis club she blew up like a bullfrog and croaked:
"That money is mine, you thief.
You stay here and I feed you.
Give it to me"
"NO!" he yelled trying to dodge her blows.

That night as Stephen sat fuming in the chicken run something happened. Suddenly he was no longer a terrified kid. At twelve years old he'd evolved into a hot-headed almost-teen. For the first time in his life he felt vicious hatred.

Next day at the club he was slow and gloomy. The guys wanted to know why.
"It's my aunt. She wants my money."
"Don't give it to her. Don't" they chorused.
What they didn't know was that Aunt-M was like the security police.

27 Night in a mango tree

The boys felt rich. They had earned well that day. They spent money on fags, booze, and drugs. Stephen puffed on cigarette buts. The boys mocked him:
"Poor Stephen, aunty will have your money."
"I don't always go home." said another boy.
"Where else could I go?" Stephen chimed in.
"I sleep under the bridge some nights.
I'm going there tonight. Come with me."

The idea grabbed Stephen but at the end of the day the boy left without him. Out of habit Stephen trudged back to Aunt-M's. He was *not* going to let her take his money. As he got near he heard her screaming. He spun away to face the night. He was afraid of being alone in the dark but staying at Aunt-M's was worse.

That night he hated everything and everyone. He didn't want to live anymore. Weird noises scared him and in a panic he scaled a mango tree.

The sky was so big and the stars brilliant. He climbed up until the leaves hid him from the sky and the ground. It was lonely and scratchy up there and cold. He could not think of anyone, anywhere who cared about him. Tears sprang to his eyes and splashed on the ground.

28 The market

The sky slowly brightened and the dawn chorus struck up cheering Stephen up a bit. He slid down the tree, looked around, saw no one, took a deep breath and made his way to the market. He watched the stalls being set up. It felt good to be around people.

A man threw out some old bananas. As soon as he disappeared Stephen grabbed and ate every bit of the discarded fruit.

He thought about the rough night in the mango tree. There were three reasons why it had been worth it. First, he was not covered in chicken muck. Secondly, he did not have to face Aunt-M and do her jobs. Most important was he still had his prized money.

Once Stephen had eaten all he could find at the market he found his second helping at the garbage bins.

29 The bridge - sleeping rough

Back at the tennis club Stephen bought fags and beer, stretched out in the sun and slept for hours. When he woke the sun was low. He couldn't face another night in a mango tree so he drifted back to Aunt-M's. As usual she treated him badly and he decided the time had come to leave for good.

The following day he explored the local bridges but slept at Aunt M's until the time was right. The next time he earned good money he resolved to spend a night under his chosen bridge. He found an empty sack in the market which would do as a blanket. The sun was sinking low as he reached the bridge. He lay down, pulled the sack over him, and shut his eyes. A chill wind whistled under the bridge. Stephen was icy cold so got up, dug a hollow in the sand, climbed in and pulled the sack over him scooping sand on top.

The stars moved slowly and silently across the big African sky. It reminded Stephen of the God at the little church he'd gone to on Sundays with his parents. The church people said that God cared for everyone. Stephen didn't think so.
"It's obvious God, you don't care for me one bit. Will I survive to be an adult or will I starve to death? I never feel well. Life is not worth living."

Stephen hardly ever cried but he did cry inside. He was always afraid, and did not see how things could get better.

By the morning he had turned a sandy coffee colour. He slipped out of his clothes, washed them and spread them on the river bank. After a swim he hid in the bushes until his clothes were dry.

At the end of the day he couldn't face being covered in sand again so he opted to share the night with Aunt-M's chickens. At least they were company and sometimes fun.

Part 4
TURBULENT TIMES

30 Beginning of the bad years

It had never occurred to Stephen that things could get worse - but they did.

He was thirteen. It was the rainy season and in the garbage bins there was only slush and maggots. Food was very scarce. Then one day Stephen's tennis shoes split. His desperate search in the bins for more shoes produced only oversized old slippers. He spent a whole afternoon working out how to tie them on with string only to discover he could not run in them.

His friends mocked him. One of the tennis ladies turned away in disgust when she saw the slippers so he ran barefoot on the courts. He had to hang in there as a ball boy as without the money he earned he would definitely starve.

At the end of each day Stephen tied on his slippers before searching for somewhere to sleep- a bridge, a tree or, if he was lucky, a partly built house.

31 Weed

The boys at the tennis club were the only people in the world that Stephen thought of as friends. They accepted him just as he was and he had begun to think of them as his family. They talked for hours and taught him all he knew, not all of it good. Sometimes he joined them smoking weed or cigarettes. He started sniffing glue. He was glad of the escape this brought. But, when he came round, his problems stared him in the face and seemed worse than before. All he wanted was to smoke pot again to escape from his fears. As soon as he had money this is exactly what he did. It was a dangerous downwards spiral.

32 The movies

"Come on Stephen, we're going to the movies." Stephen was pulled to his feet. He had never been to a movie. He did not even know what a movie was but he was happy to try something new.

The American Western was an instant hit. From the first to the last scene he lived the story. He forgot that he was Stephen, the boy with no home and no family. He was a successful cowboy!

From then on he went to the movies whenever he had enough money. It was his bit of heaven, a warm, safe place where he lived in the world of the rich. He identified with the underdogs who were always the good guys and who won in the end.

For a long time Stephen believed that everything in the movies was true. He longed to be a cowboy instead of a penniless African struggling to survive.

He would exchange his tatty slippers for shining cowboy boots and wear a leather jacket.

The fighting and violence excited Stephen and he was impressed by the way the cowboys twirled their guns around their trigger finger.
  "I'd love to own a gun," he thought.
  "I could scare people and protect myself."

33 Knife power

To survive the boys needed power. They thought that the only way to get power was through violence. Guns were hard to come by so they got hold of knives. Most of Stephen's friends had at least one knife so, as soon he'd saved enough he bought his own. He called it 'The Dragon' and decided he would put a mark on it every time he stabbed or killed someone.

The boys spent most of their time sharpening their knives and throwing them at tree trunks for practice. With every fling Stephen imagined he was aiming at someone. One day he would kill someone, and maybe more than one person.

It was the rainy season and the number of tennis players dropped off. As a result the boys were hard up. No one had enough money to buy drugs or go to the movies. Some visited their families for the first time in ages to get food.

One afternoon Stephen was more ravenous than usual. There was nothing to eat in the garbage bins so, although he had not been back to Aunt M's for a long time, he moved himself in that direction. He had sniffed glue and smoked pot that morning so felt bold but muddled.

As he got near to the house he saw Aunt-M sitting talking to someone. Ignoring the other person Stephen shuffled towards her and daringly asked for food. Aunt-M glared at him. Avoiding her angry stare Stephen glanced sideways at her visitor. He drew in a sharp breath. There was something familiar about her.
   "Why do I think I know her?"
For a few seconds their eyes locked. Aunt-M cut in:
   "Stephen, greet your mother."

Like a threatened porcupine the hairs on Stephen's back stood straight up. In all the years on his own he had missed his Mama and longed to be with her. But seeing her there well fed and fit, his love was instantly replaced by vicious hatred. His hand slipped into his pocket. He felt the deadly knife, grabbed it, flicked it open and flung it at her with colossal force.

Mama dodged. It missed her by a hog's hair as she rolled off the mat screaming:
   "Stephen!"

Stephen fled. He did not look back or stop until he reached his faraway bridge hideout. He was shaking, sobbing and searching for something that would make sense of what had happened. He

wished that he had never been born.

Stephen could not sleep. He sobbed till his sides ached adding to his pains of hunger.
"If only my aim had been better!
I can never go back to Aunt-M's.
I would be arrested and I don't want that."

34 Stephen tries to die

Stephen was fourteen. The shock of seeing his mother triggered deep despair in him. He was a survivor but after seeing Mama he had lost the will to live. He was afraid of everything and there was nobody he could turn to. No one cared about him.

Soon after the Mama-incident Stephen decided his only solution was to leave this world. He wondered if he would turn up at God's gate before he was expected. If he did, that was God's fault.

What puzzled him was *how* to die. Then he remembered scenes from the American Wild West movies. Hanging was the best way. So, he searched a building site and found some rope. He wasted no time before walking into thick bush. He stopped near the edge of the Mukuvisi River on the outskirts of Highfield, close to the place where he and his friends sometimes hid.

Stephen climbed onto a large rock next to a strong tree. He swung the rope onto a branch, slipped and almost fell. He steadied himself and paused for some final thoughts:

"No more starving and shivering.
No more problems!"

He closed his eyes and could see Mama's face as he'd thrown the knife. He was overwhelmed by the sense of loss. Hot tears rushed down his cheeks as he said his final words:

"Goodbye world."

35 Rescued

This story would have ended right here had Stephen succeeded in his plan to die.

Blackness crowded in on him. He lost consciousness. Then, through his fuzzy state he became aware that he was not alone. He heard voices:

"Boy, you could have killed yourself.
We'd better get you to the hospital real quick."

Stephen was dazed. He wasn't dead as he'd intended. Those silly women had messed up his plan! Someone grabbed one leg and someone else the other. A third took his arms. Then a strong woman picked him up, and flung him over her shoulder like a sack of potatoes. They reached the main road. That was the last he remembered.

36 Luxury lifestyle

Stephen opened his eyes. He looked about in surprise at everyone and everything. In all his fourteen years he'd never known such luxury. His first thought was:

"I must be in heaven."

He was in the casualty ward at the local hospital. Everywhere was sparkling clean and everyone was dressed in white. His attempted suicide had transported him into this astonishing luxury. Up to then he'd been sure this kind of living only happened in movies and in dreams. As soon as he was able to talk a policeman quizzed him. Stephen said nothing about Aunt-M as he did not want them to know about the knife incident. The policeman told him off then went away.

Stephen was amazed at the way people spoke gently to him. Nobody shouted. He was shown only kindness. One of the black nurses even gave him a pat on the head! A white doctor examined him carefully. The next day he brought Stephen a toy, the first he had ever had. He was afraid to play with it!

Then a shock, a bath! Stephen thought the nurses were trying to drown him. He wriggled and squirmed but every part of him was scrubbed. At first he found it embarrassing but then enjoyed it. He was dressed in pajamas and put in a real bed with crisp white sheets and propped up on two white pillows. The food was high on the list of luxuries. There were no maggots. It was always hot and plenty of it. But the knife and fork baffled him so he used his fingers.

In his two weeks in hospital Stephen was given more love and attention than he had ever known. He made friends with some of the nurses. He thought he had arrived where he was meant to be and that from then on this would be his lifestyle. But just as he was getting used to his new way of life disaster struck.

37 Campaign stay-in-hospital

Mouthwatering smells drifted up from the kitchen. Stephen lay in bed trying to guess what tasty dish would be his to eat. The nurse walked in with a tray laden with steaming hot food, put it on his side table, plumped up his pillows and said:
"We'll miss you after tomorrow, Stephen."
"What do you mean?" Alarm bells rang.
"The doctor says you are well.
You may go home tomorrow."

Stephen grabbed her arm in panic.
"No", he said desperately.
"I am not well. I am seriously ill."
"Don't be silly! You are well again."
Stephen gulped his dinner in panic. How could he solve this problem?
"I will lie still, stop joking and groan when a nurse passes."
This worked for a bit. The nurses were full of sympathy. But soon they saw through his game.

"Stephen! Quiet! No, I am not going to take your temperature. It was normal half an hour ago."

Stephen was desperate. He invented pains in his stomach, his head, chest and legs. But the next morning after breakfast the reluctant Stephen was discharged from his hospital-heaven.

38 U-turn

Stephen stood staring ahead with his back to the hospital. The old feelings of loneliness and rejection settled on him like a dark fog. He thought about his new friends, the nurses.

"They fooled me" he said out loud.
"*Nobody* cares about me, not even them.
Oh, and how I hate me too."

Stephen's self-image was rock bottom.
"I even tried to die but it didn't work.
I am no good at anything."

Suddenly his thinking changed track as he worked out a solution.
"In the movies people in prison get food. They have somewhere to sleep and company. So, I must do something bad, and get caught. Perhaps it is time I killed someone. I will be put in prison and eat and sleep until I'm killed."

Slowly Stephen strolled towards the market – he had a plan.

"First, I must steal a knife and look for a victim to kill. The police will catch me. They will take care of me until they kill me. Problem solved!"

At fourteen, with two months attempted education behind him, Stephen could see no fault with this plan.

Part 5
GANG LIFE

39 The Black Shadows

Miserable, Stephen dragged around the market with no motivation at all to make an attack. He drifted to the golf club and flopped out on the grass with his old mates. Questions flew.

"Where have you been?"
"You haven't been around for ages."
"We've missed you under the bridge."
"What do you mean?" Stephen asked puzzled.
"I decided to join you at your bridge.
At home the baby screams all night and I can't sleep!"
Another voice chimed in:
"My pa is always drunk and rank brutal.
I don't want to live there anymore.
I want to make a new life for myself so I came to share your bridge? OK?"

Stephen cheered up. That night there were four under the bridge. It was heaps better than being alone. After some days they were joined by other homeless, illiterate teenagers. All longed to belong. And so the gang started up – a substitute family.

They settled on their gang's name *The Black Shadows*. It came from the Wild West movies and sounded threatening. They modeled themselves on other gangs. They had to be fearless, frightening and tough and never show mercy, a sign of weakness. They hardly ever ventured out alone as they found this too scary. Instead, they opted for the protection of the gang. That way they felt safe, wanted and important.

They bought big knives and practiced using them on trees.

They got into muggings and break-ins, stealing knives and guns. Sometimes, when he felt really angry about white people Stephen would use a screwdriver to puncture the tires of their posh cars and scratch the paintwork.

The Black Shadows had turned into a notorious and terrifying gang. Others were asking to link up with them so they invented rules for joining.
A likely member had to be initiated and prove that he was brutal.

Just as they were trying to decide on what an applicant would have to do, a frail old lady hobbled by.
"Ah ha! Scaring an old woman would be the test."

One of the gang tried this out. He rushed at the old woman, knocked away her walking stick, and stamped on her as she fell screaming with terror. This thrilled Stephen. They ran off, not stopping until they were beyond the Machipisa Shopping Centre.

40 Violent teenagers

Most members of the Black Shadows were outcasts. They had either been abandoned by their parents who were themselves street beggars or they were orphans. They were all brutalized children who had grown into violent teenagers. They were Stephen's only friends. Their identity came from the gang. As they grew bolder, they gained control of the streets.

The first time Stephen stabbed someone it left him deeply shocked. The boy was not badly injured but Stephen was haunted by his frightened face. That night he tossed and turned and muttered in his sleep keeping everyone awake.

They guessed what was wrong and told him:

"Steve, the way to get over this is to do it again."

They were right. After a few more stabbings and then killings, it didn't bother him – at least not as much.

The gang liked paydays. They robbed and stole whatever they could.

Stephen ruled the gang. One of his rules was that women should be protected. No gang member should rape a girl or even touch her against her will. Even at that stage of his life Stephen didn't want more children produced just to land up on the streets.

41 Political tensions

Stephen was in his mid-teens. It was the late 1950s and tension was high in Rhodesia. Highfield was like a pot ready to boil over. "The country does not belong to the Whites", people kept saying. The Blacks should claim it back and rename Rhodesia, Zimbabwe.

The movement was called the Liberation Struggle and was funded by Communists outside Rhodesia. The Black Shadows were told to join the Youth League of the National Democratic Party, working for freedom.

This appealed especially to the poor, the young and the homeless. Top-secret meetings were held, in different places in the bush. People arrived one by one half an hour apart, as all meetings had been banned by the government.

Stephen went to one of the first meetings in Highfield. They were told that fighting was the only way to get freedom. They would be trained to make and use weapons - petrol bombs to damage banks, beer halls, and government places. That would make the government listen!

For months Stephen didn't join up. He did not believe anyone would want him in the Youth League. Also deep down, he was not into politics. His main worry was finding enough food to stay alive. Then two things happened that gave him the motivation to join up.

42 A muddle and a medicine-man

Stephen sauntered past the small church he'd gone to as a kid. He stopped and stood in the sun staring at the building when a man wearing a dog collar appeared. He spotted Stephen.

"What do you want here?" he said roughly.
Stephen didn't like his tone of voice.
"It's where I grew up.
My father used to preach in this church."

At once the man's manner changed. Stephen enlarged on his story. By the time he finished Dog-collar man had a picture of a devoted church-going family who had been central to his church for many years.

"Do you want work?" he asked unexpectedly.
"Oh yes!" said Stephen, pleased to be asked.
He was ready to do anything to earn money.

He followed the Dog-collar man into the church.
"These are church membership cards.
I want you to sort them into alphabetical order."
"Sure," Stephen answered, hiding his fright.

He stared at the cards. He only knew a few of the letters of the alphabet. So, for the next few hours he shuffled the cards. There was an awkward moment when Dog-collar man caught him having a fag in the church!

The next day Dog-collar man took Stephen aside.
"Stephen, I need your help. I have placed a big bet on a horse. I want to help it to win."

Stephen was curious.
"What do you want me to do?" he asked.
"Collect a black-magic potion.
You'll get it from medicine man at the race track."

A strange request thought Stephen, who was pleased to leave the muddled membership cards to themselves. He climbed carefully on to the bicycle lent by Dog-collar man.

It was a long time since he had ridden a bike but he managed to wobble his way to the Borrowdale racecourse.

The medicine man was one of the church leaders and a medicine man in his spare time! He gave Stephen a package of horse urine, horse dung, tail hairs, and a footprint of a horse in some dried mud.

"Keep this safe. And once you leave me you must not look back. Not once. If you do it will weaken the charm."

43 Double standards

When Stephen gave him the package Dog-collar man was so excited. Stephen was mystified - he was sure church people did not do black magic. So he asked him about it. Dog-collar man replied:

"For my horse to win I *must* have the potion.
But you must never tell anyone – not ever!"

Not long after this Dog-collar man discovered the mess Stephen had made of the membership cards and sacked him, shouting:
"Clear off! I don't want your shoddy work."

Stephen was glad to leave the strange man.
"The Christian God can't be great if he needs black magic to help him" he thought.
"Dog-collar man must want his people to think the power came from him."

Stephen's mind flashed back to the time his father was friendly with white missionaries.
"They invited Papa to bring us to visit them.
They made us sit outside and drink from old tins with sharp rims while all the white people used fine-looking cups.
Then they told us about their God."

Next Stephen remembered that at a National Democratic Party meeting they had been told that missionaries asked people to close their eyes and pray. While their eyes were closed the missionaries stole their land. Stephen stood bolt upright and fumed out loud:
"They've taken us for a ride."

From then on he went to that church whenever he felt like it. He liked to talk to the pretty girls in the choir and made a profit from the collection plates! He reasoned that if the leaders in that church cheated the people for profit, he could too.

44 Rage and rebellian

Then something else happened to make Stephen even madder. He bumped into a tennis lady and to his surprise she asked if he would like a job.

"My last houseboy left without telling me.
I need someone to take his place right away."
Amazed, Stephen agreed.
"When would you like me to start?"
"Tomorrow," she said.
"Come now, and I'll show you my house."

Tennis-lady lived in a luxury house. Stephen thought that he had struck gold, until they struck problems!

He had never done that kind of work before and had to be shown everything - how to iron a shirt, scrub a floor, etc. What neither Stephen nor Tennis-lady realised was that their standards were very different. Wrinkled clothes had never bothered Stephen, so if he ironed out some wrinkles he was pleased even though he added new ones! He'd only known dirt floors so, to him, the white tiled floors in the kitchen looked sparkling clean. He could not see any dirt. This made Tennis-lady mad and she told Stephen off harshly.
"I am trying, madam" he pleaded.
"You are very trying!" she snapped.

Once Tennis-lady was extra angry and said bad stuff:
"You black kaffirs are baboons.
You know that? Darwin proved it.
You lived in the trees."

This puzzled Stephen. He had never met Mr. Darwin but did not like him saying that Blacks came from baboons.

"Whites come from God." Tennis-lady finished.

The pay was stingy. Tennis-lady grumbled all day.
"She hates Blacks," Stephen realised.
What troubled him most was the way she laughed mockingly at him. He'd grown to hate her. When he could stand it no longer, he ran away leaving all the windows and doors open. He hoped she would be burgled.

Stephen had grown to hate all Whites and was ready to play his part in getting rid of them from his country. So he joined his mates at the very next meeting of the Nationalist Youth League.

45 Secret training camps

The meeting was held in a hide-out on the edge of Highfield. The small natural cave was just big enough to squeeze in ten people at a time. The leader began:
"Why are we poor and can't find jobs?
It is because of the greedy white man."
Stephen nodded.
"Do you know what to do about this?
You will never be free until you fight" he said.
"I think he's right," thought Stephen.

They were trained how to cause chaos then sent back into the townships to try out what they had learnt. For the first time in his life Stephen felt wanted.

He knew nothing about the past in his bit of Africa and nothing about the wider continent. The leaders took advantage of this. Their lessons were simple.

> "Once upon a time Blacks in Africa owned the land. The Whites came, saw the rich land and wanted it for themselves. They sent missionaries with Bibles and guns. They read from the Bible then told the people to kneel and pray. While their eyes were closed they took our land and treasures."

To prove this they showed a picture of David Livingstone holding a gun in one hand and a Bible in the other. Stephen got the point. He thought he had discovered the truth behind all the misery of his young life. From then on he hated Whites, missionaries, Christians and the Bible.

46 Preparing to stir up trouble

The lessons continued.

> "Why should you live in poverty while big houses, cars and beautiful things are owned by the Whites? These are yours by right. Are you just going to watch them enjoy your things while you starve?"

"But what can we do?" Stephen wondered.

The leader read his thoughts.

> "Only when the country is run by Blacks will there be justice and fairness. All things will belong to everyone. The cars the Whites drive are locked. When the country is ours keys will be left in the ignition. You will be able to use any car to drive wherever you want to go."

Stephen liked this idea very much.

> "I will have that white Mercedes at the golf club. Someone will shoot the owner and I'll drive it away. And yes, I'll have white Tennis-lady's house. No more sleeping under bridges for me."

47 Revenge

Stephen and crew learnt how to use small arms, make and throw petrol bombs, start riots and cause fear and chaos. The aim was to disrupt the government.

The training was tough, the discipline strict. Sometimes they were starved to get them used to hard living for the sake of duty. The Whites and all they stood for, including Christianity, would be destroyed. The leaders decided on the role of each recruit. Those who could read and write were given further training, but not Stephen. This frustrated him. He felt rejected, bitter and sorry for himself. He blamed his parents for ruining his life by abandoning him.

His trainers understood his feelings and took advantage of his anger.

"Stephen, you can do great things for the Cause. We need people like you.
Stay near to your township and cause trouble."

Stephen's frustrations grew into a craving for revenge. He would get back at those who had harmed him - the church his parents had belonged to, the Whites who lived in luxury while he had lived on their garbage.

He grew incredibly vicious. One day an educated white kid picked on him because of the holes in his trousers. In no time flat that kid was dead.

48 Chaos

It was 1960. Stephen was a trained member of the Youth League working to set Rhodesia free. The government looked on people like Stephen as Marxist thugs to be caught and shot for treason.

The task of the Youth League was to disrupt and destroy things funded by the government. They threw petrol bombs at police cars, attacked churches, and open-air gatherings. They disrupted a huge meeting in the Cyril Jennings Hall where the Prime Minister, Sir Edgar Whitehead, was due to speak. He never did! In the townships they stirred the people to violence and demonstrations.

Although Stephen was part of a tight-knit group there was very little real friendship. Everyone in the gang was filled with hatred and anger, and Stephen was no exception. The happiness they had been promised seemed slow in coming.

49 Plans to bomb a bank

May 1962. Stephen was almost twenty. It was Sunday morning and there was a huge political rally in the grounds of the Cyril Jennings Hall. Three political parties were there from Rhodesia, Zambia and Malawi. Thousands of workers opted to go out on strike for the next week to create havoc and throw the country into turmoil. They would attack anyone going to work.

Monday seemed a long way off and the restless Black Shadows gang wanted to go to the Machipisa Shopping Centre that day to petrol bomb the bank. They would set a timer so it would go off when most people were at work on Monday.

They spent that afternoon at the well-hidden cave filling bottles with petrol, adding wicks, sharpening knives and checking their guns. Then they lazed in the sun dreaming of the excitement of the coming night.

50 The tent diversion

At 6pm they left their hideout and headed for Machipisa. Suddenly one of the gang stopped.
"See that huge tent?" he said.

There in the grounds of the Dutch Reformed Church was a gigantic billowy tent. People were streaming towards it and disappearing inside. Music was playing and they could hear singing. Cars were parked nearby.

"What's that?" asked Edson, Stephen's mate.
"A circus" guessed Stephen.
"You don't have singing like that at a circus.
It sounds like a chorus to me," said another.
That was when they realised it was some kind of Christian meeting. They decided to investigate.

Edson was quick to read the sign outside the tent.
"It says Dorothea Team."
"Who are they?" Stephen asked.
"I don't know" Edson replied.
A woman nearby overheard and butted in:
"They are Christians from South Africa.
Come and hear them speak."

Stephen screwed up his face.
"Listen gang", he said.
"South Africa is a bad place. There is nothing good there. It is full of apartheid. Blacks must go here and Whites there. Whites always have the best. Why do they come here to brainwash us about their God?"
The Black Shadows nodded. Stephen continued:

"We need to teach these Christians a lesson. Tonight they'll get a lesson they'll never forget. Let's blow them up."

A few well-aimed petrol bombs would do it. People would get hurt; some would die and major damage would result. That was going to be much more exciting than throwing bombs at a bank. Besides the tent incident would give the Black Shadows a sense of power and wide respect.

51 Stephen plans a mega attack

Stephen wasted no time. He organised the gang into pairs, and told them what to do.

"We will surround the tent, two at each entrance. Stick with your partner and mix with the crowds. That way nobody will suspect you."

It was the biggest thing Stephen had planned and he wanted it to come off without a hitch.

"We will attack at 7pm. When you hear my whistle, throw your bombs inside. I want everyone in the tent to die. Got that?"

Twenty heads nodded. They hated Christians.
Stephen had not given a thought to the pain, injury and terror he would cause. His head was full of the

street cred he'd gain. None of the gangs had ever done anything on that scale.

"Remember" he warned.
"Nobody inside the tent must come out alive. If one escapes, I'll give you a bullet.
Afterwards we'll meet at the shopping center."

Stephen was a violent, emotionally crippled young man. At that time he believed every word he'd said.

George looked at his watch.
"It's five minutes to seven."
"That gives us five minutes," said Stephen.
"Let's go inside and see what's going on. We'll stay for only two minutes."

Part 6
TURNING POINT

52 A beautiful girl

People had come from miles around. Some were from Highfield. There were men in shabby trousers, women in bright dresses and pretty girls too.

Stephen's gang of twenty walked in casually and sat at the back and, to annoy people, sang loudly out of tune. A steward put his arm around Stephen's shoulder.
"Please don't sing like that" he said.
Stephen hated being touched. He spun round, pulled his knife and snarled:
"Get off! Touch me again and you'll be dead."
The steward moved away fast.

Two minutes were up. The twenty were about to leave when a man stepped onto the platform.
"Good evening. Let me introduce Rebecca Mpongose. Her life was changed on the streets of Soweto. She will tell you how she met Jesus and everything changed for the better."

A stunning girl stepped up to the microphone.
"I am Rebecca Mpongose from Soweto."
Stephen was flabbergasted. He stretched his neck to have a good look at her.
"How come a pretty girl is with these Christians? She is gorgeous."
I've just got to hear what she says."

He leant forward, listening with both ears. Rebecca spoke about a friend she called Jesus.

"When I met him, he turned my life upside down. He was so kind. His love changed everything. He forgave me for everything I'd done wrong. So I had a clean new start."

Stephen could see that Rebecca was genuine. It moved him deeply. He longed to have what she had.

"She says it is Jesus."

He remembered hearing the name Jesus when he was very young at the church his parents went to.

"Let's go," Edson whispered urgently.

Stephen felt stuck to his chair. Something strong was sweeping over him. He had seen someone who had found something he really wanted.

"Another two minutes, please."

He pulled Edson back into his seat. Edson didn't protest as he too was admiring the beautiful girl.

53 Silent preacher

Rebecca was just finishing:

"I want you to listen to Shadrach Maloka."

A tall black man in his early thirties walked slowly to the front of the platform.

It was well past seven and time to go. The Black Shadows were eager for action. But drawn by the radiance of Rebecca, Stephen sat. He wanted to find out if this preacher would say anything about the Jesus who had the devotion of a beautiful girl. He expected Shadrach to glow like Rebecca. Quite the opposite!

Slowly Shadrach moved to the microphone. For what seemed like forever he stood there staring, not saying a word. People stared back. It was creepy. Bit by bit silence fell until the slightest sniffle sounded deafening.

Without warning Shadrach thundered:
"Romans (chapter 6, verse 23) says
'The wages of sin is death. But the gift of God is eternal life.' And in the second letter to the Corinthians (chapter 8, verse 9) it says
'You know the grace of our Lord Jesus Christ. Though he was rich, for your sakes he became poor, so that you, through his poverty, might become rich.'"

Stephen jumped. A lot of people jumped.
"What a rude guy," thought Stephen.
"He didn't even say hello.
What is this Romans and Corinthians stuff?"

(Stephen was not to know that these are two letters, written by Paul the apostle, in the Bible.) He turned towards his gang and was about to give his signal. The preacher was silent again and his eyes moved like searchlights through the crowd. He did not say another word. Nothing! In the quiet, the words rang in Stephen's ears:
"The wages of sin is death. Sin is death!"

Seconds turned into minutes and still Shadrach stood in silence. Stephen said to himself:
"No one has to tell me about death.
I will die as I have lived – unloved."

Inside Stephen's mind a horror movie was playing. The script was based on everything he had ever done wrong his hatred for his family and his recent lifestyle of violence and robbery.

Then tears trickled down Shadrach's cheeks. Giant sobs racked his body. Nothing had prepared Stephen for this sight. He could not move. He felt glued to his seat.
"What's going on?" he asked Edson, who was looking just as puzzled.

54 Found out?

At last the man began to speak again very, very slowly. Every eye was fixed on him.
"I am crying because the Holy Spirit told me that many here will die tonight without Jesus."

It was as though Stephen had been struck by sledgehammer. His motive for being in that tent was to cause trouble. He was puzzled.
"Who has told this preacher about our plans? *How* does he know about our petrol bombs?"

The preacher started speaking again.
"Many of you are in grave danger.
These are violent times. You may die soon."
Shadrach repeated this many times.

Panic was rising in Stephen.
"There is no time to lose! If the preacher knows about the bombs so do the stewards. Any second now they will move towards us."
Quietly he said: "Get ready."

He fumbled in his bag to prepare his bombs and was about to tell his gang to get moving when the preacher started talking again.
"If you work for a company, that company pays you. If you work for the devil, he pays you – with death. All of you deserve the wages of the devil."

55 The pointing finger

As Shadrach boomed his threatening message, he jabbed at the crowd with an accusing finger.
"All of you have sinned. You have cheated, you have lied. You have harmed people."
Jab, jab, jab went the finger, jab, jab.

Stephen froze. The finger was pointing right at him.

"The preacher must know all about me.
Now he is telling everyone."
He whispered to Edson:
"This preacher has no manners at all.
Why does he point so?"
Edson stared at him not understanding.

The preacher continued:
"You have disobeyed God.
You think he does not see your wicked deeds.
Your tongues are full of poison like a snake."
Stephen was very nervous.
"How does he know what I did yesterday?
I kicked Robert's primus stove when it would not light. I thought nobody saw me.
This man must have chameleon eyes.
Or, Robert told him."

Stephen pulled his knife on Robert.
"How dare you tell this man my sins?
I will kill you!"
Robert jumped. He too was feeling guilty.
"Why did you tell him about me?
I will kill you too."

The preacher went on preaching and pointing. Stephen worked out how to avoid his finger. Every time the finger pointed towards him he ducked. So, bobbing up and down like a cork on a stormy sea, and with his homemade petrol bombs clanging in his bag, he felt safer.

56 Jesus

Suddenly the preacher changed the subject. He spoke tenderly about Jesus, the man who lived long ago. He was not a powerful ruler but poor and penniless. He came from an oppressed race.

"That's like me," thought Stephen.

The preacher continued:
"Jesus had no home and no money.
Nobody understood him.
He helped people and healed the sick.
His friends let him down.
He was murdered in the cruelest way.
The people he came to save killed him.
They were jealous and hated him.
They didn't know he was stronger than death.
After three days he got up from his grave.
He is still alive today."

The preacher paused.
"Because of Jesus anyone can have real life, now and always."
Then Shadrach repeated what he had started with:
"For you know the grace of our Lord Jesus Christ. ... He was rich but for your sake he became poor so that you, through his poverty, might become rich."

In a flash Stephen began to see what Christianity was about. Under his breath he muttered:
"This must be for me. Like me, Jesus suffered. He was poor and lonely, hungry and thirsty."

What surprised Stephen was Jesus did not *need* to suffer. He took it on himself to pay the price of people's bad deeds.

"Is this really true?" Stephen questioned
For the first time in his life, hope was rising.
"Can anybody have this Jesus as a friend?
The preacher seems to think so."

57 Moment of truth

Stephen stopped bobbing up and down. He was at the end of himself. He was acutely aware of his loneliness, pain, self-hatred and hate for others. Tears splashed down his cheeks. He sobbed loudly. His gang stared at him. But he no longer cared what his gang or anyone else thought.

"If Jesus *can't* take away my impossible load I no longer want to live."

Stephen wanted to be free from his terrible past, his guilt for all the bad things he had done. So with his bag of bombs, he headed towards the preacher.

"He can help me find this Jesus."
Shadrach saw Stephen's advance. He kept on preaching. As Stephen reached the front he fell to his knees, grabbed the preacher's legs, and clung on.

Strong arms seized Stephen as stewards tried to tear him away but he clung like a bloodsucker. Shadrach stopped talking and turned to the stewards:

"Leave him alone.

You are creating a disturbance."
Then he went on preaching.

58 All hell broke loose

Seconds later stones flew into the tent. Screams! Panic! A petrol bomb set a section of the tent on fire. Like a herd of stampeding buffalo, people rushed for the exits. Some were crushed. Mothers shielded their babies. There were rumbles of heavy vehicles as the police turned up. Outside was steaming with fear and violence. It was a vision from hell.

The preacher stood still with his eyes closed, trembling. Stephen knelt beside him. The team surrounded the platform and began to sing quietly. Stephen remembered that the preacher had warned that many would die that night. He wondered:
"How did he know?"

Only a few were left in the tent. The preacher turned to the young man at his feet.
"Young man, what can I do for you?"
"Can your Jesus save someone as bad as me?"
"Yes. Jesus died for you. God loves you."

Stephen fizzed and fumed. He was sure it was God who had left him to starve. He reached for his knife and said fiercely:
"Tell me again God loves me and I'll kill you."

The preacher was startled. He noticed Stephen's bag of petrol bombs and spoke softly:
"Won't you first tell me about yourself?"

It was the first time anyone had asked Stephen about himself. He poured out his story - his unhappy family; rejected by his father; the breakup of his parents' marriage; that dreadful day when his mother left him at the market place.

To Stephen's amazement the preacher began to cry. He went on crying as Stephen told him about nights under the bridge; his search for food in garbage bins; becoming a gang member; his fear of everything. The preacher listened deeply and looked at Stephen with kindness and care. That was a first for Stephen.

59 The preacher's story

When Stephen had finished talking the preacher said:
"Young man, let me tell you my story.
Many years ago there was a fourteen year old girl. She was not married but became pregnant. She did not want the baby so, when it was two weeks old, she wrapped it in a towel, stuffed it down a toilet, and ran away. A woman heard the baby's cries and found it almost drowned. She rushed the baby to hospital. Incredibly it survived. That child was me. I've never seen my mother. I don't know who my father is. Neither of them ever wanted me."
Stephen was gob-smacked.

The preacher was looking in his Bible.
"I want to read something to you.

It sums up people like you and me.
It is a promise from God to us.
It is in Psalm number 27, verse 10:
'Though my father and mother forsake me,
The Lord will take me up.'"

Those words struck a chord in Stephen.
"The Lord will take me up."
The preacher continued:
"God and Jesus are one. Jesus was God on earth."
He paused.
"My adopted name is Mohaneo, the rejected one. All through my childhood I felt rejected especially by my mother. All that changed in 1947.when I found Jesus. I was given a new name – Shadrach, after a man who lived long ago. His story is in the Bible. God saved him from huge difficulty when he was totally abandoned. I learnt that Jesus accepts me. The Lord has taken me up."

60 The load falls off

There was a great disturbance outside. The incredible fact that God loved him was sinking in. For the first time in his life Stephen knelt. He knew God was waiting for him to say something.
"God," he called out softly.
"I have nothing. I can't read or write. My parents rejected me. Take me up, God. Take me.
I am sorry for all the wrong things I have done. Jesus, forgive me and take me now."

What followed was more of a surprise to Stephen than the bombs and stones. For years he'd felt as though he was carrying a heavy load on his back. Right there he felt the load drop off. Instead of fear he felt free. He felt happiness such as he had never known before.

"I am an unwanted child like millions of others." Stephen said quietly

"But Jesus, you have found me, you want me." Something amazing had happened. Stephen felt like a brand-new person. A new life had begun!

61 The trouble outside

Stephen had forgotten the chaos outside. Others were waiting to talk to Shadrach. It was time to leave.

"I must go now," he said.

Shadrach eyed his bag of bombs. He feared Stephen might be attacked and offered to walk him to the edge of the field.

"I will be safe. In any case I am ready to die." Shadrach replied with a smile:

"Stephen, yes, you are ready to die but for the first time you are really ready to live! God bless you."

Stephen scooped up his bag of bombs and moved into the confusion outside. The scene was horrible. People were running in all directions. Bulky shapes in riot gear were moving in amongst the crowds. Bewildered, Stephen tripped over someone stretched out on the grass. His head was thrown back and his eyes open staring into space. Stephen recognised him.

"George, George, get up," he whispered urgently. But as he reached to help him to his feet, he saw that George was dead.

In shock Stephen knelt next to George. They had been close gang friends. Stephen felt guilty. If he had not gone forward when he did, it could have been him.

"I am alive and George is dead.

Why not me?" he cried in shame and agony.

Angry voices and heavy footsteps were getting close. He could be joining George in the world of the dead if he was found. He crouched, frozen, until danger was past.

Keeping low he moved off. By then his gang would have fled to safety. He stopped a long way from the tent. He found someone selling juice and quenched his thirst. For a while he wandered about aimlessly.

62 Back to the bridge

So much had happened – the meeting that morning, making bombs, setting out to bomb a bank, deciding to bomb the tent instead, and then finding God. He wanted to be alone. The hideout would be too dangerous as police were everywhere.

"I must go to the bridge.
It will be the safest place tonight."

As he walked he felt at peace for the first time in his life. He had found Jesus who was with him all way.

"My bridge" he said as he climbed up the slope. He slipped under the shelter of the bridge and dug out his bed in the sand. Tears of relief and thankfulness flowed down his cheeks
as he talked to God.

Stephen looked up at the millions of stars way above him. Gasping at their beauty he whispered:
"God, why couldn't I see this splendor before?"

Sleep escaped him. He thought about his life. After all the years of fear and loneliness, it was unbelievably good to have someone with him all the time – someone he could talk to.

Although it was only a few hours since he'd met Jesus, he wanted everyone to share in that happiness.
"God, as long as I live, I want to spend my time telling people about you."

At that moment his old fears gripped him
"Who will want to listen to me?
What good is enthusiasm without skill?"
He started to cry. Gradually his tears dried up. The night breeze seemed to blow in peace. Then he slept.

63 Hugging a tree!

Stephen woke before the dawn. He pinched himself. The events of the night before moved in his mind like a movie. The new day was going to be different. He crawled out brushing off the sand and said to God:
"Are you still there, God?"
No audible answer came but he was not alone.
"God has been with me while I slept."

He felt a totally new person – alive and well!
"I reckon I was dead and I didn't know it."

The birds were singing as Stephen went towards the river for his morning wash. To show God just how happy he was he walked up to a nearby tree and threw his arms around it.
"God, do you see me?
If you were by me I would hug you like this."
He hugged the tree again so God would get the message.

Then, without warning, Stephen heard a clear voice inside his head saying:
"Stephen. Stand up."
Stephen leapt back from the tree and looked all around. There was nobody in sight.
"Am I going crazy?" he questioned.

The voice inside his head continued:
"I will send you to nations that you do not know."
That was all.

Stephen was sure it was Jesus who had spoken to him. One day he would be sent to nations he did not know to tell people about Jesus.
"I haven't a clue how this will happen.
It doesn't matter.
I will know it when that time comes."

64 On the way to surrender

Stephen spotted his weapon-bag containing his knife and a revolver. One of the gang had stolen the revolver and given it to him as leader of *The Black Shadows.* He had no more use for weapons. He was about to throw them away when he thought someone up to no good might find them.

"I will give them to the police" he decided.

He picked up his weapon-bag, walked to the nearest bus stop, and caught a bus to town. It was Monday morning. The bus was full of gloomy commuters. Stephen couldn't keep quiet.

"Ladies and gentlemen" he said powerfully.

Do you know what happened last night?"

Heads turned and the entire bus focused on the sand-covered young man.

Above the engine roar Stephen bellowed:

"I have some really good news.

Last night I found Jesus."

There was dead silence until a large man shouted:

"QUIET! We don't preach on Mondays."

At the next stop more people piled in. Suddenly Stephen was grabbed from behind.

"It's Monday", the man shouted.

"NO preaching about the white man's god."

A thump sent him flying off the bus and face first in the dirt.

Shaken, he sat up spitting grit out of his mouth as the bus roared off in a cloud of dust.

"Preaching is a risky business" he realised.

After some time another bus arrived and he climbed on. Packed in amongst the dismal masses he could not keep quiet. He just had to tell them what had happened to him. He edged his way to the front of the bus and stood beside the driver jammed behind the large steering wheel. No one was behind his back. He was safe!

This time he decided to tell the driver. At the top of his voice, so everyone would hear, he began:
"Good morning."
The startled driver had to concentrate hard to keep the bus on the pot-holed road.
"Good morning," he replied visibly shocked.
Stephen continued:
"I have something very important to tell you.
Last night my life was changed."
"Huh?" grunted the driver.
"I found Jesus," he blurted out.
The bus swerved and headed for a ditch. With difficulty the driver straightened it up.

While every eye was on the ditch Stephen spoke. He told them about the tent meeting. This caught their attention as they had heard of the riot. To Stephen's surprise some began to cry.
"What must we do to have this Jesus?" a lady asked.

That was unexpected.
"Well, you, you…ah…you…
I don't really know.
It only happened to me last night, you see."
Stephen stammered in an attempt to apologise.

65 Kneeling on the roadside

The bus arrived in town. Stephen got out feeling upset by his failure. A small group gathered round him.

"Your Jesus has made you so happy.
Please tell us what to do so we can know him."

Stephen made a plan. He would introduce them to God and God to them, and then leave it up to God.

"Let's pray – now."
Astonishment was on every face.
"What? Here?" A woman squeaked.
"Yes. Here, now.
Let's kneel down."
"Kneel? You mean you want us to kneel?"
"Yes, kneel. Jesus died on a cross in public."
Embarrassed they sank to their knees.

Locals running for their buses tripped over them.
"What are you doing? This is not a church."
Ignoring them Stephen began talking to God.
"God, I just met these people. I told them about last night. They want to meet Jesus too."

Stephen noticed that tears were streaming down their faces. He knelt with them for a bit then remembered he was going to the police station. He picked up his weapon-bag and hurried off.

It is over forty years since the day that little gang knelt on the roadside. Stephen is still in touch with three of them who are pastors of local churches.

66 To the police station

Stephen knew where to go. He'd been there many years before as a hysterical, abandoned child. He hesitated as he reached the swing doors, hitched up his weapon-bag and walked up to reception.

"Why are you here?" a policeman asked.
Stephen's throat felt as dry as a desert in drought.
"I am under arrest."

The policeman frowned. He peered over Stephen's right shoulder and then over his left. Something was missing.
"Where is the policeman who arrested you?"

"No policeman arrested me. I belonged to the Nationalist Youth League. You never caught me but last night I met Jesus. The love of God arrested my heart so I have come to surrender."

The policeman gave him a very funny look.
"He thinks I am a nut case," thought Stephen spilling the knife and revolver on the desk.

The policeman called another policeman. He took one look at the weapons then said sharply:
"Come with me."

67 Interrogation

The senior white policeman gasped as Stephen's weapon-bag spilt onto the table. He stared at him.

"Why have you come here?" he asked.
"The love of Jesus arrested me."
"What do you mean?"
"Last night I became a Christian.
I realised I have been doing wrong."
"What have you been doing?"
"I did very bad things for the Nationalist Democratic Party Youth League."

Although Stephen was not happy with the idea of Whites ruling, he wanted to leave politics to others. He had come to renounce violence. He could easily fall into the trap of betraying his friends.

Questions continued:
"Where did you become a Christian?"
"Last night, at the Dorothea tent meeting."
The policemen grew rougher.
"Did you throw bombs?"
"No. I *was* going to throw bombs.
But I listened to the preacher and found Jesus.
Afterwards I poured my petrol into the sand.
Now here are my knife and revolver."

Someone was sent to find the preacher.
"Tell me about the Youth League?
People died last night" said the policeman.
Stephen realised he needed to be cautious.

He was ready to take any punishment but he would not grass on his friends. From then on he was on red alert to every question. He answered vaguely about his gang. He knew he would be murdered on the streets if he gave anyone away.

Everything Stephen said was taken down in writing. They wanted details of future plots, passwords, codes, etc. Stephen said very little.
"I am not very high up," he said truthfully.

68 The commissioner's parting shot

Stephen was taken to a small room, and left there on his own. He had a long time to think.

> "I am putting my life in order.
> I have not betrayed anyone.
> I have confessed all my stabbings.
> Will they lock me up forever?
> And throw the key away?"

His head chatter was interrupted by a policeman who led him back to 'the boss'.

The commissioner smiled at Stephen.
> "We have spoken to the Dorothea people.
> They say that what you have told us is true.
> So Stephen, if Jesus has forgiven you, so do we. You are free to go."

Stephen could not believe his ears. Tears spilled down his cheeks. He wiped them away with his sleeve as a policeman led him to the door.

As he was about to step outside he heard firm footsteps behind him. He turned round and saw the commissioner hurrying towards him. His heart missed a beat. In fear he thought:
"Are they going to keep me here after all?"

The commissioner looked at Stephen gently.
"Here is some money.
Go and buy yourself a Bible."

Stephen was flabbergasted.
"Yes sir. Yes sir. I will, sir.
Thank you, sir." He stammered.

He put the money in his safe pocket before floating away from the police station on cloud nine.
"I will go and find a Bible to buy.
I can't read.
But that is a small problem!" he whispered.

Part 8
VALUED

69   In search of a Bible

"Where will I find a Bible?" Stephen wondered.
"I'll try the supermarket, they sell everything."

With a swing in his step and a smile on his face he marched into the supermarket.
"I want to buy a Bible," he said.
"We don't sell Bibles," was the rough reply.

Stephen had once seen a Bible with a leather cover.
"Shoes are made of leather," he reasoned.
"I'll try a shoe shop."
So, he went into the very next shoe shop he saw.
"I want to buy a Bible," he said hopefully.
The assistant looked at him strangely.
"We sell shoes here, not Bibles!"

Next, Stephen noticed a bookshop.
"Ah ha, bookshops must sell Bibles!"
As he sprinted across the road he almost ran into a car.
"I want to buy a Bible," he panted.
"We don't sell Bibles.
But the church bookshop does."
The friendly assistant explained how to get there.

Stephen hurried off to find the church bookshop.
"Do you sell Bibles?" he asked hesitantly.
"Oh yes, of course," said the bookshop-man.
"Fantastic," said Stephen with an enormous grin.

The bookshop-man helped Stephen to choose a Bible.

With his Bible in a bag, Stephen stepped proudly out of the shop. He found a quiet corner, took his Bible out and sniffed it. It smelt new. It was written in Shona, his language. Carefully he turned over a few pages. He had no idea which was the right way up, but that, he decided, didn't matter.

"It is my very own Bible.

And proof that my life has changed."

He carefully closed his Bible, put it back it the bag, and headed for the bus stop.

70 Return to the tent

Soon after that, Stephen went looking for the tent. It was still there, and so was Shadrach Maloka. They talked for a long time.

"Life may not be easy," Shadrach warned.

"Perhaps your old gang will hassle you.

But don't worry Stephen, Jesus will help you.

He will give you strength to face every problem."

Shadrach went on:

"Everything new must grow. A baby needs milk, love and care. As a new Christian you also need food and Christian friendship."

Shadrach told Stephen of 'follow-up' meetings at a local church. He jumped at the chance and turned up at every meeting clutching his Bible. He learnt that there were three things he should do in order to grow:

→ Read the Bible every day
→ Talk to God often (called praying)
→ Meet with other Christians.

Talking to God was natural for Stephen. His problem was he could not read.

The sad day came when the Dorothea Team left to return to South Africa. Stephen felt as though he'd lost his family. Once again he was totally alone.

71 A reason for living

Stephen still lived under the bridge, and got his food from garbage bins. But the difference was that he had a purpose in life.
Wherever he went he told people about what God had done for him. His favourite places to 'preach' were on the buses and in the market place where a regular group came to listen to him.
One day someone asked why he never read from his Bible.

"Next week I will," he said.
He replied, ducking the question.

His visits to the garbage bins became less frequent as the traders sometimes gave him food and even money.

One day, Robert, of the Black Shadows, turned up. He was drifting away from the gang and grew friendly with Stephen. Robert had found a job and had his own place. Sometimes Robert shared his food with Stephen in his one-room house. They talked for hours.

"I have a purpose in life," Stephen said happily.
"It is to tell people about God."

Another day some of the Black Shadows sauntered into the market place and saw Stephen speaking. They scoffed and poked fun at him:

"Stephen's got religion. Ha! Ha! Ha!"

However, they soon left Stephen alone as they had their own chaotic problems. Many of the gang had been killed or imprisoned. The rest were afraid of what might happen to them, so they kept out of sight.

72 Let down

Stephen chose to go to a church in Highfield. He expected some sort of a welcome. But no! People were not interested in him. All he got was "Brother, God bless you" and false smiles. He felt hurt. He was used to struggling on his own but thought Christians were different, and helped each other.

When the church leaders learnt he was preaching on the buses, and in the market place, they treated him badly, calling him an 'extremist'! In spite of that, Stephen kept going to church.

One day some people, who had come to know Jesus through Stephen preaching, turned up to the church in their shabby clothes. They were immediately picked on by the church leaders:
"Why have you come here?"
"Stephen told us about Jesus.
We want to learn more," they replied eagerly.

After that the church leaders forbad Stephen to preach without their permission. For a while he obeyed but grew frustrated. He reasoned that Jesus gave him the authority to preach so he started preaching again in the market place. When the leaders found out they banned him from most church things.

Stephen was determined to stick it out, so on Sundays he turned up at church wanting to honour God and hoping to learn more.

73 A white man staring

Weeks went by. Stephen spent his days preaching on the buses and in the market place. He knew God was with him. His biggest frustration was not being able to read. One night, he called out:
"Oh! God! Open my eyes to read my Bible.
If you do I will serve you for the rest of my life."

It was a sunny day in March 1963. Stephen was standing on an orange crate talking to a small crowd about Jesus. Out of the corner of his eye he noticed a white man staring at him. It was Hannes Joubert, the man he has met at the follow up meetings. As the crowd drifted away Stephen stepped off the crate, face to face with him.

"Do you remember me?" Stephen asked.
The white man replied in Fanakalo.

(*Fanakalo is the most widely spoken mixed-up language from South Africa. It combines English, Afrikaans and Zulu. Fanakalo means: 'Do it like this.' Dramatic arm waving is used to help explain!*)

"You are Stephen Lungu. I'm so glad I've found you. I'm Hannes Joubert from the Dorothea Team. I now live in Salisbury. Shadrach told me you are a special young man and asked me to try to find you."
Stephen was deeply moved.
"I heard you preaching just now.
You are strong in your faith. Who helps you?"
Stephen looked at the ground.
"Nobody, really," he said after a long pause.
Shyly he told of the problems at the Highfield church.
"I really want to learn more about Jesus.
Who can teach me?" Stephen asked.

Hannes smiled. What Stephen heard next was beyond his highest hopes.
"I am starting a little Bible school," Hannes said.
"How would you like to be my first student?"
Stephen thought he was dreaming but quickly replied:
"Yes, yes! Yes please."

A brief handshake sealed the deal. Stephen looked at his hand to see if some white had rubbed off! He would never wash that hand again, he thought!

74 A room with three walls

"Before you make up your mind, let me show you my home," Hannes suggested.
They drove off to a small rented bungalow.

"Would you help start the school?" Hannes asked
"You are welcome to live here."
Stephen replied:
"I can't live in your house. I am a black man."
In those days, if a black man lived in a white person's house it was a criminal offence. If Stephen moved in he would have been arrested, and Hannes' Bible school would have been closed before it opened. But Hannes had a plan.

"Come and see," he said positively.
He led Stephen to the garage. It had only three walls but it was better than any place Stephen had called home. While he gazed at the garage, Hannes drove up in the van, and parked it to make a fourth wall. Then Hannes made a startling suggestion:
"Why don't you move in today?"
"What? Do you mean now?" said Stephen.
"Yes, now."
"Let us go and fetch your things."

"You mean my things?"

"Yes, your things," said Hannes.

Stephen awkwardly explained that he owned nothing except for his Bible.

"You mean you have *no things*? Nothing except the clothes you are wearing?"

"That's right," replied Stephen, feeling ashamed and wishing the ground would swallow him up.

75 Shopping spree

Hannes was not in the least put off. After a long look at Stephen he said:

"Come, we are going to town.

Stephen hesitated but Hannes was already in the van. For the next hour they shopped till they dropped. For the very first time Stephen owned his own *new* things - dark trousers; a smart green blazer; three white shirts; socks, underwear, shoes; two sheets, a blanket, towels and a steel bed with a mattress.

Back in his garage home it took Stephen fifteen minutes to settle into his new room.

Together they set up his new bed in one corner of the garage. Hannes produced a box for Stephen to store his new clothes in. Stephen carefully put his Bible on the top.

Part 9
SHOCKS AND SURPRISES

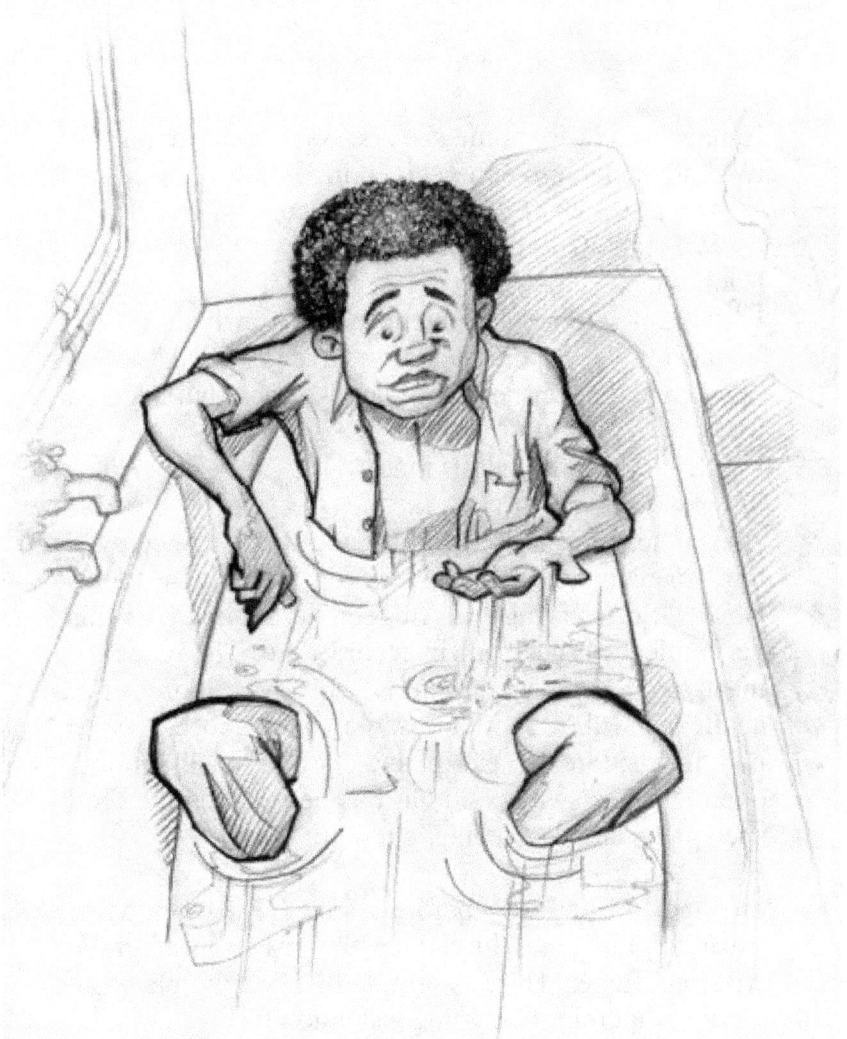

76 Culture shock

"Let's eat," said Hannes.
Stephen looked around for the house girl but there wasn't one. Hannes was the cook.

"How can this be?" Stephen asked himself.
"A white man lives in this lovely house, but there is no black woman to cook for him?"

Hannes was in for some shocks. As soon as he put the food on the table Stephen dived in.

"Stephen, wait! First we say grace.
We thank God for our food."
Hannes closed his eyes:
"Thank you God for Stephen's safe arrival.
Thank you for this food you have provided."
Stephen had never heard of 'saying grace' but he liked it.
"Get stuck in," said Hannes.

As Hannes picked up his knife and fork Stephen eyed him suspiciously. He had never used such things before. So, curving his fingers he scooped up his vegetables, eating them in record time. The chunk of meat, too big for one mouthful, was more of a challenge. Elbows on the table, he grabbed it with both hands, tore off a strip, and chewed noisily, mouth open. Hannes swallowed hard as he watched the food speeding round in Stephen's mouth.

Stephen finished way before Hannes. Not wanting to waste anything he slurped up the last drop of gravy with one finger. He was tempted to lick the plate but thought that might be going a step too far!

"Knife and fork sure slow you down," he thought. Then, to show his appreciation, he belched noisily. Hannes smiled weakly. They talked for a while in broken English and *Fanakalo*. Then Hannes said:

"Let's clear the table and wash up."

Stephen tried. He only broke one plate and a saucer!

77 Warfare with a bed!

Contented, Stephen lay awake for hours listening to the weird noises and smelling the unusual smells.

"All my problems are over," he thought happily.

Just then, he turned over in bed, hippo-style. Crash! He landed on the floor with the bed on top of him!

"This bed is fighting me," he grunted.

He righted the bed and crawled back in, lying dead still in the middle. He thought of all the rapid changes that had happened in his life and said to God:

"Thank you God. You are good to me.

I met Shadrach Maloka and found Jesus.

I promised you if I learnt to read I would spend my life telling others about you. Now at twenty I have the chance. And I have a home."

His last thoughts before falling asleep were:

"The future looks exciting.

I will learn to read and get to know Jesus better."

For once life seemed uncomplicated. But nothing on this planet is quite that simple!

78 A bizarre bath

Stephen woke full of hope. He dragged on his old clothes, keeping his new ones for special occasions, and hurried to the main house. Hannes was in the kitchen cooking. Puzzled at what he saw and trying to disguise the dismay he felt, he said:

"Come with me, Stephen."

He opened the bathroom door, ran the hot water then sent Stephen to fetch the clothes they'd bought. When Stephen returned with his new clothes, Hannes pointed firmly to the soap, and the bath, and left Stephen to it.

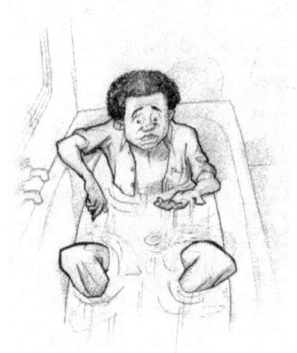

Carefully Stephen climbed into the slippery tub. His clothes stuck to his body. He soaped them all over but when he got out he found it hard to pull them off. He slapped them against the bath splashing everywhere.

Hannes gulped at the state of his first student and the bathroom. He pointed to Stephen's wet things, led him to the line in the garden, and told him to hang them up to dry.

"A man should not have to hang up washing," Stephen was thinking.

Things got worse. Stephen almost rebelled as Hannes led him to the bathroom and gave him a mop. After a long time it was clean.

"You wash clothes outside and yourself in the bath," Hannes explained.

Stephen cringed but cheered up as they ate breakfast, celebrating his first lesson at the Bible school!

79 Tricky training

The time had come for Hannes to discover the level of his first student. Stephen's spirits sank into his new shoes as paper, pencils and books appeared. Hannes soon realised that his only pupil was illiterate. On the plus side he had faith in Jesus, enthusiasm, and could speak in broken English. His vocabulary was mainly to do with golf and tennis.

A lesser person than Hannes would have given up, but he was tough. He believed God had helped him to find Stephen, and that he wanted him to start a Bible school. So, he talked his problems over with God:

> "God, I have no money, no building, no teachers, hardly any books and my first pupil is an illiterate twenty-year-old. He lived under a bridge and has Marxist ideas. What he knows about Christianity is from the tent meeting that he intended to bomb. Oh God, this is all too much. Help!"

Hannes realised he would have to civilise Stephen, teach him table manners, and how to read and write. First he'd have to support, encourage and help him to grow in his faith. Then he would put him through Bible school.

It was a long haul starting that day.

80 Mountain tops and valleys

Sometimes everything seems to be on your side. You think you know where you are going. You catch a glimpse of the mountain top you are heading for, but don't realise you must first travel through the foothills. Soon you find yourself on a slippery slope going down, down, down into a deep valley. You can no longer see the mountain. The way is hard, the journey long. You wonder why you ever started.

This happened to Stephen. Compared to his old life he was in clover. He had left behind poverty, crime, fear and loneliness. But not everything was rosy.

> "Hannes expects too much," he grumbled.
> "I like running my own life. He is a control-freak! He tells me when to get up and when to go to bed. I must make my bed, wash every day, and do women's works like housework. Hannes wants me in when I want to be outside. I must learn the English alphabet, how to spell and read and write. It's boring! It's not me."

At the start of each day Hannes inspected the garage.
> "Why is one shoe under the bed and the other by the door? Fold your clothes. Take off muddy boots before you walk inside. Plates belong in the kitchen, not under your bed!"

On and on this went. Then they'd have breakfast.

To give Stephen reading practice Hannes asked him to read to Josias Ngara, a blind local preacher, who hoped to join the Bible School. They had loads of fun.

81 Breakfast bits and sound bites

Breakfast was full of more training sound bites.
"Stephen, don't chew with your mouth open. Cut your meat if it is too big for one bite. Hold your fork in your left hand, your knife in your right. Ask, don't stretch. Chew quietly. Say please."

Years later Stephen thought back on those days and wondered how Hannes had survived!

Hannes told Stephen about the Dorothea Team. It was started by Christians, for the poor and homeless people in South Africa. Later they realised there were also people in the same situation in Rhodesia. That's why they held the tent meeting. The Bible School, *Soteria* (A Greek word meaning rescue), was part of their plan. Stephen was the first student. Hannes was Stephen's 'personal tutor' and taught him about Jesus.

When Jesus was thirty he started teaching about God. After only three years, he was killed. His murderers thought they had got rid of Jesus for good. But no! After three days Jesus walked out of his grave, alive and well. Then, for forty days thousands of people saw him. Many believed. They were called Christians.

There was a man named Saul who hated Christians and had killed many. One day Saul was dramatically changed. He was his way from Jerusalem to Damascus to arrest Christians when he was blinded by a brilliant light, and struck to the ground. He heard a powerful voice:
"Saul, Saul, why are you persecuting me?"

It was Jesus speaking. For three days Saul was blind. But he had found God, and spent the rest of his life telling people about Jesus. He had a new name – Paul.

"I am like Paul," Stephen twigged.
"I planned to kill Christians by bombing a tent. Instead, I met Jesus.
Now I have landed a life-long job."

82 Soap-less

There were not many rules at Soteria but they had to keep to certain principles. The most important was '*Walk in the light*' which meant keeping a clean slate with everyone. There were to be no grudges. When things went wrong, they should be sorted out quickly. Stephen found this easy while only he and Hannes worked together.

The principle to '*Live by faith*' Stephen found harder. No one was paid anything. They had to ask God, and trust him to supply what they needed. Hannes was personally penniless. Much to Stephen's surprise, things usually worked out. Local farmers supplied much of their food and others dropped in with provisions. One day Stephen asked:
"Do you tell people what we need?"
"No, I never do!" Hannes said firmly.
"You must never tell anyone except God.
Telling people what we need is like begging."

Then Stephen found they were almost out of soap.
"Hannes, we need a new soap in the bathroom."
"I haven't got one."
Eagerly Stephen said:
"If you give me the money I'll buy one."
"I haven't got any money," replied Hannes".
"Tell God we need soap and leave it to him."
With that Hannes went out. Stephen fumed:
"Asking God for a bar of soap is ridiculous.
Surely God has more important things to do?"

The next morning, as Stephen was having a wash, the last sliver of soap disappeared down the plughole. He was desperate so turned to God.
"Please God, send us some soap."
That afternoon while Hannes out, there was a knock at the door. As Stephen opened it, a large paper bag was thrust into his arms.
"I can't stop! Take this," said the glowing lady.
"I went shopping this afternoon and thought these groceries might come in handy for you two."
With that she was gone.

Stephen dived into the bag, pulling out one item after another. At the bottom were two large bars of soap.
"Oh God, you heard me!" Stephen whooped.
He leapt about the kitchen in a victory dance. Just then Hannes walked in. He realised Stephen had not gone totally mad once he heard the soap story!
"Stephen, it is not the soap itself that counts. God honours those who trust him for their needs. This is his way of showing you. It is right to work for money but God is teaching you to trust in him."

Stephen never forgot that lesson.

83 Holes in his soles

Stephen made a big mistake. He told someone what he needed. That someone gave it to him. But he felt bad as though he had cheated God. So, he plucked up the courage and told Hannes. He was forgiven.

Soon Stephen needed something else. Shoes! When he walked the soles of his feet touched the ground. He put cardboard inside but that only worked for a few minutes. He didn't even tell Hannes. His new self-confidence seemed to drain out through those soles. Everything was difficult, every day. No money. No shoes. No let up from study. He felt hemmed in on every side. He was discouraged.

"I will never win," he thought.
"I've had enough.
I've got to get out of this place."

He packed his things in the box and wondered where to go - the bridge; back to daily fear? Hopeless! His only option was to keep going. He stared at the floor.

Helping Hannes prepare for new students was a long hard job. They cleaned, scrubbed, scraped, puttied, painted, and put in extra boards and windows until the old chicken runs in the back yard, became bedrooms.

Stephen learnt new skills, but his shoe crisis got worse.

84 A surprising solution

Dorothea visitors came on their way to Kenya. They were a cheerful lot. Stephen liked them. His fear and self-hatred seemed to disappear. One day Thomas Barlow invited Stephen to go to town with him.

"Sure, I'll come with you," Stephen replied.
He was shy of Thomas, the son of a wealthy white businessman. But the thought of getting out of lessons proved stronger than his shyness.

"Where would you like to go?" Stephen asked
"Where do you want to go," said Thomas.
I want to buy you something, but I don't know what you want - trousers, shirts or shoes?"
"Shoes," Stephen gasped.

There followed a shopping spree to beat all shopping sprees. When they got home Stephen owned three pairs of trousers, two pairs of shoes and a smart suit. After the Dorothea visitors left Stephen told Hannes:

"I only asked God for shoes," Hannes beamed but said nothing.

New student Lucy Phiri was the first to arrive. Lucy couldn't read or write and Hannes couldn't understand her. So, Stephen got his first job as interpreter Three months later Nelson Phiri, Lucy's husband came. He had worked for a sugar refinery. Ex-gang member Moffat Ncube joined them. He came from Bulawayo. He and Stephen hit it off big time. And there was less washing up to do since they all took turns.

Around that time Hannes got married to Sustine, a delightful young woman from South Africa.

85 Dodging death

Stephen sat mulling over the terrifying dangers he had faced in the past few years with the Dorothea Team.

Stoned in Rhodesia

"It was 1965 and at the start of a big tent meeting. It became obvious that the people were hostile, so we decided to leave. As we reached our van a rock-storm broke. A brick just missed my head but smashed the driver's knee. At first he couldn't drive. Then I yelled at him to move, as we didn't want to be dead meat. Just in time we got safely to the police station."

The funny side

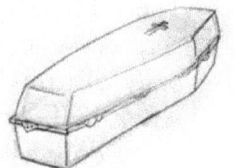

"The next morning, when I was out of town, my cousins decided I must have died. They told my aunts who immediately started planning a huge funeral! When I turned up my aunts grumbled: 'That boy was always unreliable!'"

Scary incident in Zambia

"On another occasion I was working with Shadrach Maloka in a market place. People were jittery. I wanted to quit but Shadrach started preaching. Then the angry mob rushed at us, shredded our Bibles, and destroyed our sound equipment. They grabbed Shadrach and tossed him between them like a rag doll. I tried to stop them but they beat me up then stoned the car where other team members were sitting. I wanted to fight back but I heard a voice saying: 'Stephen, stop fighting. Kneel and pray.' As I did the police turned up and rescued us."

Stephen went on thinking about his past dangers.

Near murder in Malawi

"We were staying in a village near to Blantyre, and had gone to bed after a long day. Suddenly I was woken by a deafening banging at the door. It was a gang of angry violent men, from the Youth League.

'Come with us,' they commanded.'

We were marched into the bush, hands tied behind our backs. They said they would tie us up in sacks and throw us into the river. I thought I was about to die but when I remembered that Jesus had died for me I reasoned that dying would be O.K."

"Suddenly, we came across a camouflaged hideout. Asleep on the floor, snoring like a wild boar was the Malawi Congress Leader. Startled he woke up. 'What are these men's crimes?' he asked. When he learnt it was preaching, he roared:

'Do you want to fight with God?
Untie these men and let them go.'"

"Wearily we walked back to the village arriving around dawn. To our surprise hundreds of people had spent the whole night praying for our safety. Everyone was happy and thanked God for His protection."

118

Part 10
TOUGH TRAINING

86 High standards

A major change was taking place in the Dorothea. Headquarters had sent Patrick Johnstone, a clever English man in his twenties, to lead the Rhodesian team. Hannes still ran the Soteria Bible School.

Stephen looked forward to a new start.
"It will be a lot easier with Patrick.
I can read and write. And use a knife and fork.
I am so civilized that I hardly know myself!"

Patrick was interested in everyone. For the first six months he spent time getting to know them all, their skills, strengths and weaknesses. He loved the Bible, God's guidelines for living. As far as Stephen could tell, Patrick knew every word on every page. Patrick wanted everyone in his team to know the Bible well and so become effective workers for God.

When Patrick lived in South Africa most Whites thought they were better than Blacks and were always in charge. Patrick hated this. He believed God had made all people equal, each with a special job to do. His aim was to train Africans as leaders in all walks of life. With Patrick's guidance, Stephen saw that he had the chance to become the person God wanted him to be. This made him very happy.

What Stephen did not know was a massive challenge lay ahead. He would be taken apart and put back together again. It would cost him pain, tears and effort. At times he would want to run away.

87 Breaking cultural barriers

Patrick was determined to pull Stephen up to his level. It gave Stephen a lot of grief! Patrick spent more time with him than with the other students, often inviting him to a meal in his caravan. They talked for hours.

One morning Patrick told Stephen that they would go visiting together.
"I can't do that.
It won't work," protested Stephen
"Yes it will," Patrick insisted.

Stephen's confidence hit rock bottom. The shyness he'd known under the bridge rushed back.
"Patrick, I can't go into a white person's house."
"Yes you can."
"What will I say to them? They won't want me."
"They will. We'll give it a try. God did not make a mistake when he made you. You are as good as anyone. You've just had fewer chances."
Stephen had no option. Later they went visiting.

Patrick knocked on the door. A white man appeared. Stephen stood behind Patrick, eyes glued to the ground. Then, Patrick introduced him as an equal:
"I'd like you to meet Stephen Lungu from the Soteria Bible School."

The white man looked pleased but Stephen was so busy looking at the ground he did not notice.
"Good day, sir," he managed to say.
Patrick glared at him. Slowly Stephen raised his head and looked the white man in the eye.
"Do come in. I'll get something to eat and drink."

Stephen's eyes returned to the floor as he slunk into a chair in the corner. When alone Patrick got stuck in:
> "Stephen, sit back. Relax! Don't wind your legs in a tight knot; stretch them out in front of you. You've got a great smile Stephen – use it."

Relaxing was impossible at that point. When the white man came back Stephen was wearing a fixed grin and was sitting bolt upright

Every time they went visiting Patrick picked on him:
> "Stephen, don't shuffle. Shoulders back."

Once, as they were leaving a house, Stephen bowed. Patrick went wild and gave Stephen a silent thump.
> "Stephen, NO. He is not a king.
> He is just a man like you and me.
> Walk tall - none of this bowing and scraping."

It dawned on Stephen that, bit by bit, Patrick was pulling him up to be the person God made him to be.
> "Patrick is a man in a million," he whispered.

88 Working routines

At Dorothea it was most important that everyone should be close to God, study the Bible, and tell others about Jesus. For the next thirteen years, as the team moved from one venue to another Stephen's daily routine was:

Mornings time alone with God; prepare for the day.

Afternoons work locally. Evenings meet in the tent. There were many details to remember like getting an official invitation from local churches, and permission from the police. Tents and chairs had to be found; local helpers trained and music planned.

Stephen had developed a talent for playing the piano-accordion so he was in popular demand. He got one day off a week. Usually he spent it sleeping! His basic needs were provided but there was no salary. Yet he felt happy and contented.

89 *A stand against injustice*

Patrick had visitors from the Dorothea headquarters ('The-Dotties'). Unfortunately for Stephen, they were the 'racist' kind of South Africans. Soon they were on to Stephen.

"Stephen, it is rude to call Mr. Johnstone, Patrick." Later that day, when they were all having tea with Patrick, Stephen needed to give him an urgent message. He cleared his throat and said timidly:

"Mr. Johnstone,"
No response from Patrick.
"Perhaps he didn't hear me," thought Stephen.
"Mr. Johnstone" he said a little louder:
Still there was no response.
The message was important so Stephen blurted out:
"Patrick!"
"Steve."

Patrick turned to him with a smile

That was when it dawned on Stephen that Patrick was giving The-Dotties a strong message. He loved Patrick that day. The-Dotties left the room in a huff!

The next day Patrick went out. He'd hardly gone when The-Dotties pounced on Stephen.
"Stephen, it is your duty to wash our cars, clean our shoes, and sweep the place while we are here."

Stephen was embarrassed. He had always done those things for Patrick and Hannes, but they treated him with respect. When Patrick's muddy van arrived Stephen stepped up with a bucket of water.
"I've come to wash your van."
Patrick stared at The-Dotties. In a loud voice he said:
"Nonsense, Steve! I made it dirty. I will wash it."

As The-Dotties left the next day their last words to Patrick were:
"Stephen is on a slippery slope dabbling with Marxism."

That stuff with The-Dotties made Stephen realise how much Patrick was doing for him. He danced a little jig of joy. But Stephen's jubilation was to be short lived.

90 Pressure, pressure, pressure!

Patrick moved to Bulawayo, a large city in the southern part of Rhodesia. Stephen often spent weeks with him. He had grown up a lot and become a more rounded person - socially, mentally, emotionally and spiritually. He was surprised by his improvement. However, all was not blue sky and sunshine. A crisis was brewing like a billowing storm cloud.

Stephen grumbled to himself:
"Patrick keeps nagging me. He has me on a winch.
Every day he winds it up a bit tighter.
He never lets me rest."
When Patrick wasn't working on Stephen's English, he was teaching him basic book keeping.
"Stephen, read the newspapers, books, the Bible.
Your pronunciation is poor. Say it like this."

It was work, work and more work! Stephen felt like Jack in the saying 'all work and no play makes Jack a dull boy'. He could never relax and be himself. Rebellion mounted.
"Patrick is always picking on me.
He seems to think I must be perfect."

Time keeping was a big issue! In Africa people are more relaxed about time, but Patrick did not seem to know this. Sometimes he ticked Stephen off in front of the other students. It made Stephen embarrassed.
"Stephen, nine o'clock is not eleven o'clock."

It annoyed Stephen that when other students arrived half an hour late Patrick said nothing.

91 Enough is enough!

One day Stephen nearly killed himself to be on time but arrived ten minutes late. Patrick snapped:
"Stephen, *when* will you learn?"

Stephen was furious. It was the last straw. Seething with resentment he left and went to his room.
"I hate Patrick.
Patrick hates me too.
I've had enough!"
He jam-packed all his stuff into a box and stalked out.
"I'm gone.
I will go back to Salisbury."

But this was not to be. He heard high-speed footsteps behind him. Patrick caught him up half way down the street.
"Where do you think you are going?
And after all I've put into you. I won't let you go.
Your place is here.
You should try harder."

Patrick almost dragged him back.
"Stephen, you are going to be the best you can be,
if it kills us both in the process!"

Stephen did not doubt Patrick meant every word.

Daily frictions went on. Patrick and Stephen were very different people. Stephen acted on his emotions. Patrick was a man of careful thought. So, they often got on each other's nerves. At night, Stephen told all his troubles to his pillow:

> "Patrick is such a harsh man.
> I can't live up to his standards.
> However did I get into this place?"

What saved the day for Stephen was the weather. The rainy season ended and the team was able to get out and about again doing what Stephen liked best – telling people about Jesus.

Part 11
LOVE AND MARRIAGE

92 Lonesome

By the late 1960s Stephen could mix with anyone and had friends in many countries. He and Patrick were on good terms. He was really satisfied with life. Or was he? He was in his late twenties and longed for a wife. In Africa it was unheard of for a man of his age to be single. But he could see a lot of problems.

> "How can I marry? I have no money. I have a job but no salary. All I own fits into one suitcase!
> I don't want to marry any of the girls I know. Even if I find someone would she want me?

Stephen had a deep fear of failure because of his parent's broken marriage. So, he said to God:
> "If you want me to marry, please prepare me."

93 The recurring dream

One day Stephen had a waking vision. An attractive young woman was sitting in front of him, wearing a loose blue outfit, holding a Bible upside down open at the book of Acts, chapter 26.

That chapter is special to Stephen as it is about the turning point in the life of Saul, who became Paul, the apostle. Paul had set out to throw Christians into prison. Stephen had set on out to kill Christians by burning down the tent. God had stopped Saul and had stopped Stephen. They had both been turned around.

Over the next two years, Stephen had exactly the same dream twice more. What could it mean?

94 Learning to drive

You never know where one step forward will lead.

Out of the blue Patrick came out with:
"Stephen, why don't you learn to drive?"
The familiar hollow feeling rushed back inside him.
"No. What if I crash? The van is expensive."
Patrick ignored Stephen's protests. Driving lessons started straight away. The first lesson was a disaster. The car took off like a bucking bronco.
"Don't grind the gears. Not so fast!
There is no raging rhino chasing you," Patrick said severely.

After a few sessions Patrick was happy with Stephen's driving. He just needed practice so Patrick got Stephen to drive through the middle of Salisbury. Then, to Stephen's surprise, Patrick announced:
"Lungu, you are a natural. Congratulations!"
Stephen's confidence went flying sky high.
"I am a driver," he said, hardly believing it.

95 The girl in blue

Stephen's new skill was to change his life. Soon after he'd passed his test, a friend asked him to drive him and his two daughters to Malawi. The girls were booked in to a boarding school.

With Patrick's blessing off they went. After dropping off the girls in Lilongwe they set off for home. In Blantyre they stopped to visit a friend and were invited to stay for Christmas. As they sat around talking someone mentioned a remarkable young girl who worked at Barclay's Bank.

"In her lunch breaks she is out on the streets telling people about Jesus. She is just like you Stephen. You should meet her."

A few days later Stephen spoke at a youth rally. Afterwards, he was talking to a man named John.

"Can we meet again at my home?" John asked.
Then, out of the corner of his eye, something, or rather someone grabbed Stephen's attention, a girl wearing a loose blue dress and holding a Bible upside down, open at Acts, chapter 26. Stephen shivered.

"She's the girl in my dreams. What is this about?"
He knew the answer.

The next day was Christmas day. After the church service Stephen set out to visit John, but John had gone out. Just then John's sister appeared. Stephen gasped. She was the girl of his dreams!

"Hello, I'm Stephen Lungu," he said shyly.
"I know, I heard you speaking last night. I'm Rachel. Sorry my brother isn't here. Come in."

Stephen did not have the courage to talk to Rachel just then. His head was spinning.
"Tell John I will call back soon."

Stephen was on cloud-ninety-nine as he walked towards his Christmas dinner. He just couldn't stop thinking about Rachel.
"How I can meet her again?" he wondered.

96   Christmas proposal

Stephen stood rooted to the spot at the entrance to the Christmas dining room. Was he seeing things? No there she was again, sitting at the table, the girl of his dreams. During the meal Stephen hardly spoke. He was trying to work out what he would say to Rachel when they were alone. His biggest worry was:
"If I ask her to marry me, what will she say?"

Stephen normally had a good appetite but hardly ate a thing. Eventually the meal came to an end. He wasted no time in inviting Rachel to join him for a walk.

Before they had gone very far Rachel asked:
"Stephen, please tell me your life-story."
Stephen hid nothing. He told her about his unhappy childhood, his lack of education, years sleeping under the bridge, the Black Shadows, and his plans to bomb the tent. Rachel took it all in.
"You had no schooling?" she asked, amazed.

As they talked Stephen realised that Rachel really understood him. She was the one for him and he could not hide those thoughts any longer.

"Rachel, we've only just met, but I love you. Would you honour me by becoming my wife?"

Surprised by the out-of-the-blue marriage proposal Rachel gently responded:

"Stephen thanks for your offer. I need time to think, and to talk to God. It is a big decision."

Stephen's heart did a somersault. She hadn't said no!

"Rachel, take as long as you need." He replied.

As soon as he got back to Salisbury he sat down and wrote Rachel a letter. That year, the two of them heavily sponsored the post office! Stephen was so glad that Hannes had taught him write!

A year later, in December 1968, Stephen set out to visit Rachel.

"I have no home and no salary to offer her.

But I can look my very best," he thought.

So, he packed *all* his clothes and caught the bus bound for Malawi. Disaster! His suitcase was stolen. Once again his Bible and the clothes he was wearing were all he owned. Stephen felt very sorry for himself.

"Rachel will never want me now."

97 Rachel's answer

Stephen hurried round to Rachel's home. The family pelted him with questions. Eventually he and Rachel managed to escape for a walk alone. Stephen spoke:
"Rachel, have you thought about..."
Before he could finish she looked up at him:
"Yes, Stephen, I have. I will marry you."

Those words sent Stephen into a roller-coaster spin.
"No Rachel, I don't think you should.
Have you thought about what it would mean?
You would have to give up your job and leave your lovely home, and friends, just for a poorly educated man who can't give you anything."
Rachel was taken aback.
"But Stephen …"
Stephen interrupted:
"I have no money, nothing, not even a bed."
"Stephen …"
"Rachel, even my suitcase was stolen.
No, Rachel, I can't marry you," he said firmly.

Rachel burst out laughing. She put her pointing finger on Stephen's lips.
"Stephen, listen!
I am not planning to marry a bed.
I am not planning to marry a house.
I am not planning to marry posh clothes.
No! I am going to marry *you*."

Gently he took her hand and kissed her fingers.
"I am looking at a miracle.
This woman loves me just because I am me."

98 Objections

Back home they announced their engagement. Rachel's family was appalled especially her uncles. They seemed stuck on Stephen's violent past. To have him as a son-in-law was going too far.

"Rachel what if he wants you to throw bombs?"
Rachel was mildly amused.
"Uncle, I don't think that is possible."
"We don't want you living under a bridge."

Stephen wasn't exactly feeling wanted. He sank into a sofa. At that moment Rachel's mother came in.

> "Mother, meet Stephen Lungu the man I told you about. He's the one I want to marry."

Rachel's mother beamed, and in an un-African way strode across the room, knelt in front of Stephen, took his hands and said:

> "Stephen let's talk to God: 'God thank you for Stephen and his love for Rachel. He is welcome in our family. Stephen, you will not be my son-in-law, you will be my son."

Stephen and Rachel wasted no time. They decided to get married on December 20, a year since they'd met. Preparations began in a flurry. Stephen expected it to be an easy and happy few weeks. But it turned into one of his biggest nightmares.

> "First problem, I do not own a suit and Rachel's mother says our marriage won't be legal unless I wear one. What can I do?"

Days before the wedding someone gave him a suit.
"Problem solved!" Stephen said gratefully.

99 The wedding cake

The next problem surfaced the day before the wedding. Rachel's mother cornered Stephen:
"Stephen, it is your job to provide a wedding cake. You can't have a wedding without one."
Wide eyed he replied:
"I do not know this custom."

Stephen panicked. He had no money to buy anything. Desperate, he walked into the bush.
"God, I need this cake. Please sort this out."

When he got home he found an envelope waiting for him post-marked Salisbury, but no sender's name. Inside was £80, exactly what he needed to buy a wedding cake. In awe, he sank to his knees:

Stephen shot off to the wedding cake shop.
"I want to buy a wedding cake today," he said
"Impossible! Cakes must be ordered weeks beforehand."
Thinking quickly, Stephen pointed to a large cake:
"Can I have one of those cakes instead?"
"No! You can't serve *that* to wedding guests."

That night he hardly slept. Early on his wedding morning he was back at the shop.
"Mr. Lungu, those people you passed outside this shop just cancelled the wedding cake they ordered for today. It's yours if you want it?

The cake was delivered to the uncles who took it safely to the wedding reception!

100 At the church

Stephen arrived early. As they went into the church Stephen noticed that his Best Man was looking rather green. They were standing at the front waiting for the bride to arrive, when all of a sudden there was an alarming crash.

The Best Man had collapsed on the floor at Stephen's feet. Guests rushed up to help and in next to no time the Best Man was on his way to hospital.

Just then the bride arrived with her parents. Stephen was terrified. "Will they think I've poisoned my best man?"

The minister smoothed things over and got on with the wedding ceremony. At last he said:
"I pronounce Stephen and Rachel man and wife."

Stephen and Rachel walked down the aisle relaxed and smiling. The reception was a roaring success. And the cake, people said, was the best they had ever tasted!

101 Honeymoon hazard

Stephen and Rachel spent the first few days of their honeymoon in Salima, a town near Lake Malawi. Then they moved to a tiny house in Blantyre that belonged to Rachel's sister. It was seven foot by seven foot! The bed took up nearly all the space - their wardrobe was a suitcase stored under the bed.

After a few days Stephen fell seriously ill with malaria. Rachel thought he might die. But slowly he recovered and when he was well enough he went back to Salisbury. Rachel followed later.

Rachel made a huge difference to Stephen's life. He put on weight and always left home looking smart.
"My wife is everything a man could want. She is like an anchor and makes me feel secure."

Rachel was well educated and could talk to anyone. Stephen admired this but sometimes it caused him grief. One night, after Patrick had told him off, he saw Patrick smiling and talking to Rachel. His heart sank.

Rachel chatted all the way home. Stephen was silent.
"Why did I marry this clever woman? She is too good for me. Will I be able to keep her love?"
Rachel slipped her slim fingers into Stephen's.
"What is wrong, Stephen?" she asked gently.
Stephen could not hide anything from her. Rachel laughed when he told her his thoughts.
"Stephen you are a silly old thing! I had the chance to marry bank managers. I *chose* you."
Stephen cheered up. A weight rolled off his back.

102 Nothing to eat

Stephen earned very little and sometimes they ran out of food. The first time that happened he'd been away. As he arrived home he sensed something was wrong.

"Stephen, I'm so sorry," Rachel said sadly.
"Today I am like Old Mother Hubbard. The cupboard is bare and I have nothing to cook."

Stephen was embarrassed. His thoughts went like this:
"I have let Rachel down. I should bring in the money to buy our food. But hang on a minute…
I have just been telling people to trust God to provide for them. I must put this into practice! Rachel," he said.
"We must ask God to organise food for us."
So they did. Then Rachel set the table.
"What are you doing?" Stephen blurted out.
"Why do you ask?" Rachel replied in surprise.
"We have just put in a request to God for food!"

Two hours later the doorbell rang. They were greeted by two huge bags resting on top of a pair of legs. Two eyes peered at them through the gap in the bags:
"Hello, you two. God told me to buy you some food. There is also a little money at the bottom.
I must be off now. I have lots to do today."
With that she disappeared. Rachel wasted no time in preparing a luxury meal.

There were many times when they ran out of something. It became their habit to ask God to provide. Sometimes it was clothing, sometimes food. God never let them down.

103 The banker

Rachel had worked at Barclays Bank before they got married and was good with money, so Stephen appointed her as family finance manager. This created a stir amongst her friends - it was unheard of then for a woman to manage her husband's money.

> "How did you do it? Did you use black magic? Give us the recipe!" Rachel's friends asked.
> "No black magic. The secret is in the Bible. It teaches you the best way to live." Rachel replied.

Many women became interested in God and told their husbands. Before long Stephen and Rachel were helping couples work through marriage difficulties. From then on they worked together to provide marriage guidance.

104 Walking the floor

Stephen stared at the perfect bundle in Rachel's arms.
> "Can this lovely little girl, Agnes, be my child?"

They were new parents. Everything changed. Agnes needed love and care all day and all night. Stephen got lots of free advice especially from Patrick of course!
> "Stephen, you must help look after Agnes."
> "What? Babies are a woman's job."

> "Rachel is not your housekeeper she is part of you as your wife. By helping to look after Agnes you show your love for Rachel."

Many nights Stephen walked the floor rocking his baby. He was even on nappy-washing duty. It gave Rachel a chance to catch up on sleep. What surprised Stephen was, because they cared for their baby together, they grew closer. A big plus was getting to know Agnes at the start of her life.

In the stillness of the night Stephen had time to think. His childhood came flooding back, the lack of love, the loneliness, the hunger and the harsh conditions. Self pity rose to the surface until Stephen remembered how God had rescued him again and again.

Agnes squirmed in his arms. She was restless. He gave her a cuddle to settle her.

Then new thoughts crossed his mind:
> "My parents were not capable of loving me as their lives were too messed up. That's why they deserted me. They are somewhere out there and don't know they have a granddaughter."

Part 12
DEALING WITH THE PAST

105 The trap

Patrick's wife, Jill, was a gentle, caring person. She loved African people and whenever there was a rub between Patrick and Stephen she sorted it out.

One day at breakfast Patrick gave Stephen one of his 'something-is-coming' looks.
   "We can have more meetings.
   Where would you like these to be?"
   "Mpopoma Township," Stephen suggested.
   "Good idea Stephen, this time you will do the organising."
Stephen groaned inwardly.
   "I have walked straight into this Patrick-trap."

Then he blurted out a long string of 'why-nots'.
   "I can't. That is impossible!"
   "Nonsense," Patrick said firmly.
Stephen broke into a sweat.
   "I am not educated.
   I can't write letters.
   I can't speak to the police.
   I'm no good at organising."
   "Yes you can, and you will do this Stephen.
   I know you can do it."

Patrick had made up his mind and Stephen knew it. That night Stephen had a long talk with his pillow.

106 Visiting the police

Next morning Patrick was quick off the mark.
"First we write to the police."
Stephen felt that old knot tighten in his stomach.
"The police won't want to hear from a Black."
"Nonsense, Stephen! Write it."
"I can't."
"Get on with it!"

Stephen wrote slowly. After a long time he showed the letter to Patrick. Patrick's face fell.
"This is appalling," he said, tearing it into shreds.
Almost choking with frustration Stephen suggested:
"Patrick, you must write."
"No, but I'll show you how. Copy what I write."
Stephen copied it. Patrick tore up version two!
"Patrick, why did you do that?"
"I couldn't read it!"

The next morning they started again and finally a sort of letter was ready.
"Stephen, take this letter to the police."
"No, they will want a white person."
"You will go, and go on your own Stephen.
When you get there say what you want straight away. Don't waffle on about anything else."

Stephen was terrified. At the police station he forgot his English. He stammered and stuttered and couldn't look the man in the eye. Back at base he told Patrick:
"He said no."

"Go back and insist," was Patrick's hard reply.
When Stephen returned the next time he was smiling.

"He said yes!"
Patrick beamed. In that way, bit by bit, Patrick helped Stephen to conquer his inferiority complex.

107 The bombshell

Things were running smoothly. Stephen was used to going to the police to get permission for their meetings. Then, one Sunday, as they were enjoying one of Jill's delicious dinners, Patrick calmly announced:
"Steve I have a message for you.
You are invited to preach at the English Church."
Stephen was transfixed. It was as though he'd been hit by a bombshell.

Patrick wasn't joking. So, for the next ten days Stephen sweated over his talk. He was terrified of speaking to a white congregation. He planned to speak in Shona, his mother tongue. Patrick would just have to interpret.

Stephen was pleased with his talk until, on the Friday before he was due to speak, Patrick asked to see what he had written. Patrick tore it up. Stephen was horror-struck.
"No. He wailed. Why did you do that?"
"You are speaking in English!"
All Saturday Stephen struggled with his talk. He didn't eat. He spent all the time trying to re-write it.

"God, do you know that Patrick is so unfair?
He is determined to embarrass me.
What must I do?"

Stephen got to the big church early. As it filled up he felt like running away. Silently he cried to God for help.

His time had come. Knees knocking, hands shaking, and voice wobbling, he began. When he got to the bit where he was holding his petrol bombs, and walking down the aisle, he forgot to be nervous. He told about the incredible longing for God that had swept over him, and about preaching on the buses and meeting Hannes and then Patrick. At that point he ran out of English so sat down.

The church was silent until Stephen heard hushed sobbing. He had never seen Whites cry.

108 Speaking to thousands

To help Stephen in future, when he spoke in English, Jill and Patrick talked through all his mistakes. At the very end Patrick congratulated him.
  "Stephen you are a good communicator.
  You have a remarkable story to tell.
  Your love of God shines through.
  You did well."

Stephen wasn't often praised by Patrick but, before he could dwell on this, Patrick was on to him again.

"Stephen, from now on, every day you should read the newspapers and books in English."

In the years that followed Stephen spoke to thousands of people in central and southern Africa.

In 1975 Patrick took Stephen to Mozambique where he was spokesman to the governor of Beira. As usual Stephen was afraid, and not keen to do this, but he did it! Permission was granted to hold meetings. Stephen was pleased. But he did wonder what was coming next. Patrick always had more in mind for him.

109 Drunken old woman

The year was 1976. Stephen was working in a Salisbury township. The day had been tough, with six open-air meetings. He was ready for home. He switched off the microphone and turned to leave but something was pulling on his trouser leg. It wasn't something but someone holding him back. A little old woman was grasping his trousers. She stood in front of the platform staring up at him in a strange way.

Stephen crouched down. The stench of stale alcohol hit him. She was ill, a skinny drunken mess.

"I want to pray with you," she said forcefully. Stephen could not face it.

"I will call a women counselor to pray with you."
"No, I want *you* to pray with me."

Stephen realised the only way to disentangle himself from her was to give in. He knelt down next to her. He had hardly started praying when she leapt up and danced around saying:

"My pain has gone.
I want to give my life to Jesus."

Stephen prayed with her again. Then she prayed – on and on. He slumped against the platform but the miracle of this woman finding peace with God kept him awake. Finally she turned to Stephen. He smiled. Clearly she needed help, he thought, while trying to unravel himself from her grip on his sleeve.

"Come back tomorrow night?" he suggested.
At that she burst out:
"Do you know that you are my son?"

110 Falling apart

Stephen could not take it in. She repeated:
"You *are* my son. We lived in Highfield, me, you, John, and baby Malesi. Remember?"

A shock wave hit Stephen with the force of a tsunami. He was falling apart. Memories flooded in on fast rewind. The nightmare of those days filled his mind-screen. One question after another flooded his brain.

"Is this shriveled up woman really my Mama?
Why did she leave us? We could have died.
Where did she go? Why? Why? Why?"

The waves of the aftershock struck.
"I hate you Mama."
Stephen thought he'd forgiven her years ago but he hadn't – not completely.
"I still feel like I felt that day I threw my knife at you. I hate you, Stephen thought"

Then, Stephen recognised a still small voice saying:
"Don't abandon her.
She is your mother.
She needs you now.
She has found you, and through you, she has found me. Take care of her for me, my son."

The woman clearly needed help. Her present husband, a Muslim, beat her daily. Stephen made plans to meet her the next day.

111 Listening

Through his mind fog Stephen eventually found his way home. At first he could not speak. He just sank onto the bed like a jelly fish out of water then started sobbing.
Rachel wrapped him up in her arms.
"Stephen what's the matter? Are you ill? Tell me."

"Rachel, I…"

"What happened?"

At first he just could not say the word 'Mama'. Then, slowly his story came out.

"I found my Mama."

"You did what? Where? Is she alive?"

"She came to the meeting tonight."

Rachel listened intently as his story unfolded.

What happened in the days that followed was stranger than fiction. They invited Stephen's mother to come to live with them. After she arrived Rachel, although heavily pregnant, treated her like royalty, attending to her every need. She bathed and deloused her, burnt all her clothes and gave her new ones. She kept her away from the beer that harmed her. Stephen was amazed at Rachel's care of his tatty old mother.

"What a wonderful wife, a living saint!"

When Mama had recovered enough Rachel got ladies from the church to befriend and care for her. With all the love and attention she progressed rapidly.

Stephen kept his distance. Being near his Mama was too painful. He had too many questions he could not ask. Why, what, when, where and how spun in his head. Then, some weeks after Mama arrived, there was a breakthrough. Stephen was alone with her enjoying the afternoon sunshine. They got talking.

"When did you marry this husband?"

"It was after I got back from Bulawayo."

"What were you doing in Bulawayo?"

"Brewing beer… I was with some friends. That was where I went after…"

Stephen was struck by another shock wave.

"How could my mother dump me to brew beer?"

That night Stephen wept hysterically as he told Rachel. Rachel listened and tried to comfort her crumpled husband. Then her wisdom surfaced.

"Stephen there is another side to this story. Mama was only a child when she was forced to marry your father. She tried running away but her parents always sent her back. She had nowhere to go. By nineteen she had you three children. I think all this made her depressed. It was all too much for her so she ran away."

Stephen did not understand that. His work began to suffer and he felt ill so he asked Patrick for time off.

112 Into the bush

Stephen disappeared into the bush on a dark night. As many Africans do when in trouble he went there to sort himself out. For three days he wandered around with a churning mind and heavy heart. He badly wanted to forgive his mother but just couldn't. Stephen was deeply damaged by the loneliness, rejection and fears of his childhood. He didn't eat. Again and again he begged God for help and healing. On the third day something amazing happened.

"I felt a heavy weight lifted from my shoulders. The fog of bitterness and resentment cleared. Suddenly I could see Mama as a helpless old woman shaped by her own damaged childhood. I no longer hated her. Actually I began to love her. This was God's doing, not mine."

It was there in the bush, that long buried memories had surfaced. Like the day when Mama had abandoned them and the hate-giant first invaded his life. And times at the orphanage, when a teacher had thrashed him brutally, and he had bottled up his pain, anger and resentment. Those negative emotions had imprisoned him. At last he'd broken free. Stephen went home filled with energy and love to an overjoyed Rachel. He had new zeal for telling others the Good News. The Church grew.

It was late in the 1970s. Mama had been with them for two years. The time had come for her to move into a little home of her own. Stephen and Rachel were glad of the extra space as their family was growing. By then they had three children of their own and an unwanted baby that they had taken in.

Mama blossomed. Her faith grew strong. For three years she studied at the *Soteria* Bible School, training as a children's worker. After her training, Mama and Stephen sometimes spoke in public together. He found it was fun to introduce Mama as 'my spiritual daughter'. For two years she worked in Zambia with the Dorothea Team. Stephen was overjoyed.

"What a transformation! Only you could do this, God. Something beautiful has emerged."

113 Life in Malawi

In 1978 the Lungu family moved to Malawi as Stephen was to head up a new Dorothea Team there.

> "This is an incredible honour." Stephen reflected.
> "I am Dorothea's first Black leader.
> I love Malawi and I'm half Malawian.
> And this is Rachel's country too."

They moved in with Rachel's mother in Blantyre. Parents, kids and clobber squeezed into one room. Stephen became busy working in Malawi and beyond.

In the rainy season he and Rachel ran Bible study groups together. When the group grew to twenty they split it into two. People from all over the city joined. Lives were changed for the better.

Stephen employed two helpers. He bought them each a little house, but he, Rachel and kids stayed living with Rachel's mother, all Lungus in one room.

Stephen explained:
"I don't want to live better than my workers."

114 Seven in the bed!

The older you get the faster the years seem to fly! Three years had sped by since the Lungu's moved to Malawi. Stephen's work flourished.

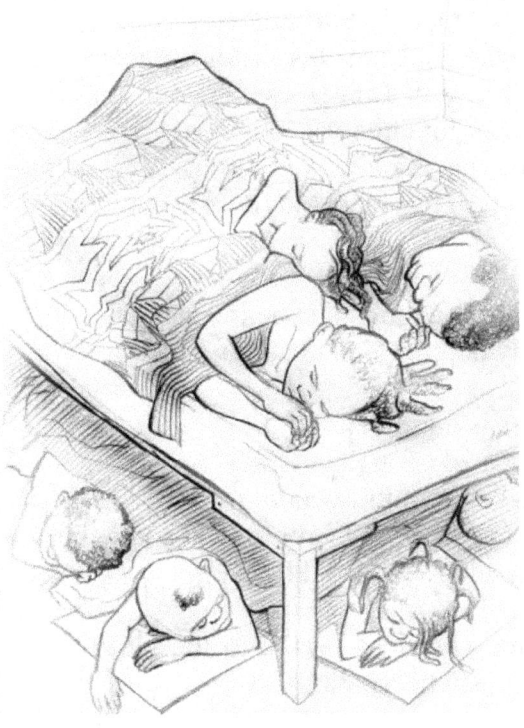

In all that time Stephen, Rachel and kids continued to share one room. The oldest slept in the bed with their parents. The younger ones were rolled in blankets and tucked under the bed.

Then, in 1981 Rachel had another baby. It was getting overcrowded!

In the late spring Stephen went to a huge meeting in Malawi led by Michael Cassidy, a well-known evangelist from South Africa, and founder of African Enterprise (AE). (AE's aim is to evangelist the cities of Africa through word and in deed, in partnership with the church.) Michael needed a good translator. As Stephen spoke both Shona and English well, he was Michael's man. The minute they stepped onto the platform together they became a great team. They had the same enthusiasm for telling people about Jesus. Afterwards Michael asked Stephen to take him to the Dorothea Malawi HQ so they could talk in private. As they drew up outside the house Stephen explained:

"Malawi HQ is in one room.
It doubles as a bedroom for seven Lungus!
It will be easier to talk in the car."

Michael tried hard to hide his astonishment. So, cramped in the little Volkswagen Beetle he listened to Stephen's story. His potential was obvious.

"Stephen, you have only worked in Africa but your work could go wider. Maybe AE could help you."

"Is he offering me a job?" Stephen wondered.
I am out of my depth. I'd better fill him in."

"I doubt if this is possible."
"I am not educated enough.
I've only had two month's schooling.
I was over twenty when I learnt to read and write.
I need time to talk to God and Rachel."

"Take the time you need. Write to me when you have decided." Michael said.

The next day Michael was gone.

Stephen felt as though he was on a see-saw! One minute he was up, wanting to take up the challenge, the next he was down in inadequate-land. What should he do?

115 The strange ways of women

After a few days Stephen could keep quiet no longer.
"Rachel, there are things I must tell you. We all like it here and my work is going well. However, I'm nearly fourty and I can't stop thinking that it is time for a change and a fresh challenge."

He went on to tell her about his time with Michael.
"Rachel, you won't believe this! I think Michael is going to offer me a job at AE. Then we will have our own house and I will get a salary."

Rachel was indignant.
"Stephen we can't do this! Dorothea has done so much for you. We must stick by them."

Stephen was astonished.
"Rachel isn't even attracted by the prospect of having her own home. End of subject."

Crushed, he crept away to consult God.
"God, Rachel says no!
If a move to AE is your plan, you must tell her."

Stephen had already written to Patrick to ask his advice. He ripped open the reply as soon as it arrived.
"Go for it," Patrick had written.

But Rachel wasn't for shifting and Stephen got on with his job, which meant being away from home for long periods. When he returned Rachel was waiting.

"Stephen we must go," she said.
Startled Stephen asked:

"Go where? Has your mother thrown us out?"
"No! We must join African Enterprise."
Stephen stared at her open mouthed.
"Why does Rachel start a serious conversation as soon as I walk in the door feeling dog tired?"

Stephen flopped into a chair outside. The children brought him a cool drink.
"Rachel, why have you changed your mind?
What's happened?"
Looking surprised Rachel replied:
"Nothing has happened!
I just know that we must."

Stephen could get nothing else out of her. But one thing was clear. Rachel was just as convinced that they should join AE as she'd been against it earlier.

116 Surprise reminder

Something propelled Stephen into action. He was in a boring church service and, to relieve his irritation, he reached for his Bible. It opened on his knee at Isaiah 55 and a line stood out on the page.

'I will send you to nations that you do not know.'

Stephen almost dropped his Bible.
"Where have I heard these words before?"

Visions of his home under the bridge flashed through his mind. He recalled hugging that tree and afterwards hearing a voice saying:

"I will send you to nations that you do not know."

It was not Stephen's habit to dip into the Bible picking verses to prove a point. But what he had just read he knew was from God.

"God," he asked silently.

"What are these nations?"

No audible answer, but the words African Enterprise popped into his head.

That night Stephen could not sleep. He and Rachel lay in the dark whispering about the significance of that Bible incident for hours. In the glow of the candlelight Stephen could see deep happiness on Rachel's face.

The next day he wrote to Michael Cassidy in his very best Patrick-style handwriting. Michael replied immediately. He enclosed a plane ticket, and an invitation to Stephen to attend an interview in Nairobi, in January 1982.

117 The interview

Stephen looked smart. He arrived in good time. He had never had an interview before and was nervous. Then he saw another guy also waiting to be interviewed. That was extra scary.

Before Stephen even had a chance to sit down that smart-guy told him all about himself. He was from Ghana and well educated. He had done loads of things that would appeal to AE. Instantly Stephen's hope of getting the job flew out of the window.
"Why did they bother to bring me here?
They will choose this smart-guy.
I might as well go home right now."
He found a table-tennis ball and bounced it nonstop.

The Ghanaian was called in for interview and seemed to be in there forever. Then it was Stephen's turn. He was shaking like a leaf in a strong wind.
"I am not good enough. It's hopeless!"

After general questions the Board asked him to tell them about his life. Stephen perked up. He was confident on this subject. He told them about his childhood, teenage years under the bridge, his gang, and the tent meeting when he met Jesus, and how his life had changed. He went on to his years with Dorothea and how he had been helped.

His interview was over. Back in the waiting room he retrieved his ball and gave it plenty of exercise! After a while the door opened and a lady came out with the decision letters. As the Ghanaian guy read his, his face fell:
"Sorry no - maybe at a later date."

Stephen stuffed his unopened letter into his bag.
"Why bother to read it?
I know what it says.
They have turned down smart-guy so they won't want me. I will have to apologise to Rachel. She

was right the first time. We belong with the Dorothea people."

Stephen rushed out and onto the next plane.

Rachel met him at the door with a look of expectation.
   "Well?
   "No. They said no."
   "That's crazy!
   They invited you. What went wrong?"
Looking peeved Stephen explained:
   "Michael invited me but the Board decides.
   They said no."

With that Stephen said he had errands to do and handed Rachel the letter.
   "But Stephen you haven't opened it."
   "I hate failing," he said as he rushed out.

When Stephen returned some hours later Rachel was standing in the doorway waving the letter. With a big smile she said:
   "You are a crazy, crazy man."
   "You've got the job!
   It says so in the letter."

Part 13
TOP JOB

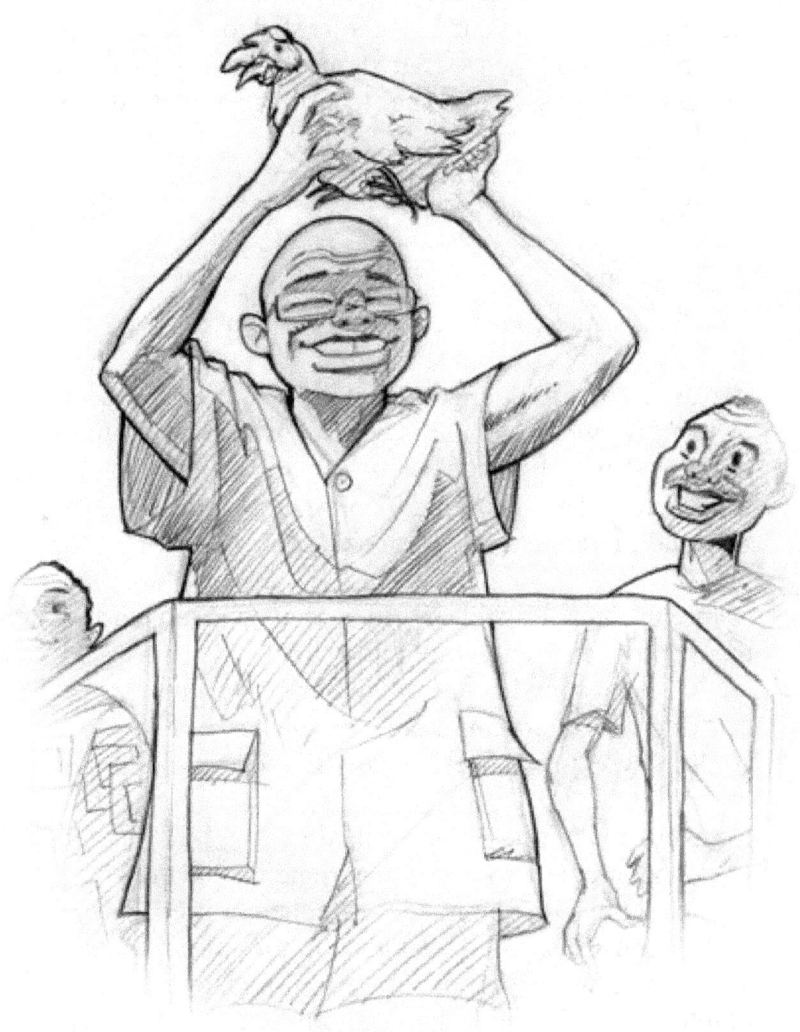

118 House hunting

It was a big step for Stephen but time to move on. He had worked for Dorothea for nineteen years.

He met the AE team in their spacious office in Salisbury, and then went house hunting without success. Chris Sewell, the team leader, raised his eyebrows:
"Why are you looking in the townships?"
"Where else should I look?"
"In AE we don't believe in segregation.
You will live in an AE owned house."
So, Chris sent someone else to find a house.

It was a cheerful bungalow, with a large garden, in Eastlea. By white standards it was not so classy, but to Stephen it was a palace! What would Rachel think he wondered? Then the thought crossed his mind:
"Did I ever get food from *this* garbage bin?"

A month later, Rachel and kids arrived. Stephen met them and in excitement told her:
"I've just found a house like ours in Malawi."
"Can we go straight there?" Rachel asked.
"First you must meet my new friend."

He drove to the house and walked in.
"What are you doing? Your friend is not here?"
"He told us to wait inside." Stephen bluffed.
"He must be posh. Hey kids don't touch anything." Rachel said wearily as they raced through every room. Stephen could keep up the bluff no longer. He grabbed Rachel and shouted:

"This is *our* home! Welcome Lungus!"
Rachel was speechless. She wondered around in a daze. The kids went crazy.

"Will we really sleep in our own beds?
No more rolling us up in blankets under yours?
Is the garden ours to play in?"
"Come now!" Stephen said filling the kettle.
"I think your mother needs a cup of tea."

119 Tear gas and a gang leader

Stephen's job title was 'Evangelist'. He loved it. Every day he could do what he liked best of all, telling people about Jesus.

One day Stephen and Chris Sewell were talking about the past. Chris told Stephen of a narrow escape he'd had as Chief Inspector Detective in the Rhodesian security police. He was protecting the Prime Minister, Sir Edgar Whitehead, when a violent gang had set out to stone him.

"I had to use tear gas to disperse that gang."
Chris recalled.
Stephen was taken aback.
"I was the leader of that gang," he confessed.
Incredible!
That was the start of a strong friendship.

120 To nations you do not know

After a few months with African Enterprise Stephen was invited to America. As the plane landed in New York he checked his watch.

"It seems like we left Europe hours ago but the announcement makes it only two!"

He didn't know about time zones!

As he left the airport white stuff was falling from the sky and everything, everywhere, was white.

"What is that?" he asked.

"Snow – you must have heard of snow!"

At 2.00 am he was still wide awake. He had not heard of jet lag either! Three culture shocks in a row!

The Americans worked him hard. For six weeks he spoke five times a day to students, young wives, business men, churches etc. His story touched many.

Over the years Stephen had travelled to Australia, New Zealand, Canada, Argentina, the Middle East and Europe – Switzerland, Belgium, Holland, and the UK. In Africa he was in demand from Cape Town to Cairo.

He spoke in townships, cities, slum areas, mines, football grounds; prisons, posh hotels and police stations - to business men, factory-workers, fishermen and Presidents. Nobody was too insignificant or too important for Stephen. Wherever he went he found people, from all walks of life, who were without hope and sometimes in despair. He always pointed them to the best hope he knew, Jesus.

121 A chicken highlight

Stephen has always loved chickens! There was one chicken he met in a rather unusual and special way.

He was with African Enterprise in the city of Monrovia, Liberia. They were working with the local churches, in a slum area of 20,000 people known as the 'Buzzi Quarter'. Stephen was the main preacher.

The closing rally was at the Samvu Doc Stadium.

The Vice President of Liberia arrived in his motorcade with sirens blaring. To show his appreciation of the work of the Monrovian churches, in partnership with African Enterprise, he ceremonially presented Stephen with some Koro nuts and a chicken!

122 Old man under a tree

It was 1986 when Stephen heard the news. Papa was alive and living near Blantyre. With the help of local chiefs Stephen and Rachel found him.

There he was, a very old man sitting under a tree sucking on sugar cane. The chief introduced Stephen. He barely recognised his father. For a while they stared at each other, the old man, fear in his eyes, thought Stephen was a policeman! Slowly a flicker of recognition came:
"I remember. You are little Stephen."
Father and son were both in tears.

Stephen felt no bitterness, only sadness for this poor old man. Gradually he pieced together Papa's story. He had married again twice. His present wife was ninety.

In 1991 Papa's wife died. Stephen and Rachel invited the 'old man' to live with them. For nearly eight years Rachel looked after him like her own father.

One day Papa was lying across Stephen's lap. Papa spoke:
   "My son, thank you very much for finding me and for forgiving me."
Stephen replied.
   "That's just what Jesus did for us."
His old Papa, then 104, said:
   "My son, may I pray for you?"
That is what Papa did.

At the end of his prayer they both said 'Amen'. Papa never opened his eyes again. He had left this earth to be with his Jesus.

123 Thirty-year secret

Stephen was on the African Enterprise mission team to Durban, South Africa. He had no idea that it would provide a missing piece of his life's jigsaw. That day he was the stand-in preacher at a little mixed race Durban church as the person due to preach was ill.

Everyone was spellbound as he told the story of his miserable young life. He had got as far as the tent episode when two little old ladies started whispering excitedly to each other. At first Stephen ignored them. Then they left their seats and shuffled towards him:

> "Young man, we must tell you something."
> "Can't this wait until I have finished preaching?"
> "NO. We must tell you now."

All eyes were on those two little disturbances. Stephen felt defeated! In thirty years of preaching he had been stoned, jeered at and mocked, people had tried to run him down. Never before had he been ambushed by two old ladies in their Sunday best!

With a sigh he stepped off the stage towards them.
> "God gave us *you*. We have it written in this Bible. We prayed for you that day."

They thrust their Bible into Stephen's hands. In the margin, dated 14 May 1962, was written:
> "Jesus, will you save one gang leader tonight."

Stephen was astounded.

> "I never saw you in the tent."
> "Of course not, we were here in Durban.

>We knew about the Dorothea meetings.
>We asked God for one gang leader.
>Now we know God answered."

Stephen was in tears. The old ladies were in tears. Then everybody was in tears. Stephen was so caught up in that amazing life drama that he even forgot to ask their names. It was the only time he met the two ladies who held that vital link in his life-chain.

124 The new millennium

The whole world was watching the clock tick out the last minutes of the twentieth century. But some, like a guilt-ridden accountant in Lilongwe, whose wife had just found out about his affairs, were desperate.

At 2.00am on 1 January 2000 the phone rang.

>"Mr. Lungu, I am going to kill myself."
>"Who are you?" asked Stephen, waking up fast.
>"Life has nothing for me," sobbed the man.
>"Can we meet?" Stephen suggested.

The man was there in 15 minutes, leaving his wife trembling in the car with the engine running.

Stephen and Rachel talked with them for the rest of the night, a long story. For the couple it was the best possible start for the new millennium. They had hope for their future. They had discovered Jesus, who had forgiven them, and they had forgiven each other.

So, that is how the Lungus greeted the New Millennium. Very tired but satisfied, they went back to sleep.

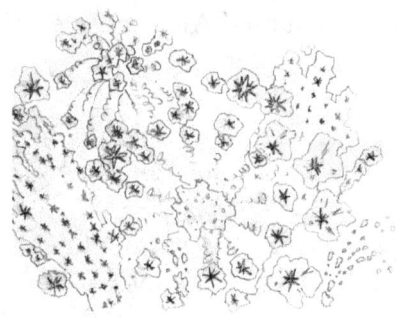

125 Top job

It was 14 May 2002, forty years since Stephen's remarkable tent-experience. Looking back he was jubilant. He had been changed from a lost, ragged, violent nobody to a valued somebody.

Fear and frustration had been replaced by freedom and fulfillment. He had a wonderful marriage, friends in many places and thirteen children (five of his and Rachel's own), and grandchildren. He loved his hectic job as leader of the African Enterprise Malawian team. So, he puzzled about the feeling that God had something more for him to do.

Meanwhile Michael Cassidy, African Enterprise's founder and International Team Leader, was due to retire in 2005. AE was looking for his successor. The short list got shorter and shorter until there was only one candidate left standing – Stephen Lungu.

So that was it! God did have something more for him to do. Michael congratulated Stephen warmly saying:
> "I want to give you my life verse. God gave this to me when I started African Enterprise. It comes from Joshua chapter 1:

'As I was with Moses, so I will be with you. I will never leave you nor abandon you.'"

Stephen was overwhelmed but confident. If God was with him, and this was God's job for him, he could go anywhere.

126 A secret behind this story

Truth is far, far stranger than fiction. And so it is with the Stephen Lungu Story.

Who could predict that Stephen, with his tough background of rejection and violence would eventually be at the helm of a large Christian organisation with teams in ten African Countries, and support offices scattered around the world?

Who would have thought that a totally illiterate and uncouth young man of twenty, whose self-confidence hardly ever got above ground level, would one day be in demand as a speaker around the world?

How was it possible for a man who hated God, South Africa and Whites to become the leader of a great Christian evangelistic organisation that had grown out of South Africa through the inspiration and leadership of a white man?

Yes, truth *is* stranger than fiction! For it is not fiction but fact that in the tent that night Stephen met Jesus. He was turned upside down and became a new man. When he returned to his bridge, and noticed the splendor of the stars, for the first time in his life he knew he was not alone.

Ever since, he has walked with God. The icy rejection of his youth has been replaced by warmth, acceptance and love.

Stephen never stopped smiling and spreading this light, love and hope. And if you had met him he may have told you this:

> "*Nothing* is impossible with God.
> You don't need to be a victim of your past.
> You too can find a friend in Jesus and start again.
> Instead of fear, anxiety, and loneliness your life can be one of faith, hope and love.
> God bless you."

Stephen's message for you

I often wonder about you kids out there who may be under a bridge, or under someone's veranda, or sleeping in an old car, with no blankets to keep you warm. Perhaps you are saying: "I wish I had a dad and a mother. I wish I had food to eat."

I also think about you kids in the Western World. Perhaps you have lots of things but no love in your life. Perhaps you are from a broken home. Perhaps your parents are not there for you, or treat you badly. Is your best friend the TV or computer games? Are you feeling lonely and lost and don't know why you are here? Do you sometimes think that life is not worth living?

I understand. I've been there, and I want tell you this:
    I found hope, in a hopeless situation.
    I found help, when all seemed helpless.
    I found life, laughter and love when I discovered I was loved by the man called Jesus.

As you read this book remember, you have a friend who understands and is praying for you.

Stephen Lungu

Hear Stephen speak

To hear Stephen speak search Stephen Lungu on You Tube. He is a born story teller and an amusing communicator. There are numerous versions of his life testimony as well as, for example, his teaching on aspects of the Bible.

Read Stephen's books

Out of the Black Shadows – Autobiography.
The amazing transformation of Stephen Lungu, Stephen Lungu with Anne Coomes (see Amazon)
ISBN 9780825460258

Take Me Up – Stephen Lungu
Christian Focus Publications
ISBN 1527108260, 9781527 108264

A brief history of Stephen Lungu

Stephen is seen here with the author in 2018

The product of a dysfunctional family, he got involved with street gangs. Angry at having been abandoned by his family, and at the white government he led his gang to blow up a Christian Tent meeting. Instead he gave his life to Jesus!

Uneducated and illiterate he was taken under the wing of Patrick Johnstone, a British missionary, who educated him. After working with the Dorothea Mission, he was invited to join African Enterprise later succeeding Michael Cassidy as AE's second International Team Leader.

Thank YOU

Stephen Lungu, Street Kid turned Evangelist. It is for his life, laughter, humility, and unswerving love and faith in Jesus, together with his inspiration and guidance in bringing this book into print, that I am thankful.

Michael Cassidy, founder of African Enterprise (AE) 1962, Stephen's predecessor as AE International Team Leader and CEO, thank you, for your direction and encouragement.

Stephen Bowley, my late husband and my brick. I am thankful he stood by me all the way, and for the title of this book: *From a Street Kid*

Adam and David Bowley, our kids, for your insights and various forms of help, thank you.

Sybil Parry (d. 2010) remembered for her faith in this project, and constant encouragement.

Thank you to my writer's Team:
Grace Townshend, Bill Baxter, Bev Quarterman
and to all who commented on various drafts
Deborah Hennessy, Hilary White, Joan Boughton, Jill Ewbank, Sandra Pillay, Meshack Khosa., Chris Trent, Leanne and Chris Kelly, Jean van Rensburg, Carol Cassidy, Malcolm Graham, Olave Snelling, Teenager Tasha.

Anne Coomes, who assisted Stephen in writing his autobiography:
OUT OF THE BLACK SHADOWS.
Thank you for the opportunity to use this as my main source of reference.

Niko Petropouleas, your sketches bring the book to life, **Louis de Jager** (front cover image)

In gratitude

African Enterprise,
(AE) founded by **Michael Cassidy** in 1962, has advanced the Gospel throughout Africa.

Result:
Positive change and HOPE for multitudes.

The Bible
Nothing is impossible with God (Luke 1:37)

Jesus, the friend who loves says:
I will never leave you nor forsake you
(Hebrews 13:5)

Contact

AE South Africa
aesa@ae.org.za

AE International
www.aeint.org

Last words

Why I wrote this version of Stephen Lungu's life

A few years back I was reading *Out of the Black Shadows*. Stephen's autobiography. Words leapt from the page. I recognised that the feelings of rejection, worthlessness, and despair that Stephen experienced, when he was growing up, were not unique to him. Kids all over the world go through these crises. Many, in our virtual, media-driven world, never read a 'dense-print' book so, I concluded, Stephen Lungu's story would have to be told in a simplified format to be accessible to these kids. And, as Michael Cassidy, founder of African Enterprise has since said:

Stephen's story is a modern chapter from the book of Acts and deserves to be widely read.

On that day, in my study, the next thing I read was from the book of Joel in the Bible – chapter 1, verse 3:
*Tell this to your children,
and let your children tell it to their children,
and their children to the next generation* (NIV).

Could it be that God was telling *me* to write a simplified version for the younger generation, and those who don't like reading much? Some months later I met Stephen and talked through my vision. Here you have the result!

It is my prayer that through these pages many will be shifted from despair to hope. It is after all not just the story of Stephen Lungu's surprising turn around, but an example of the amazing love of God for everyone.

About the author

Born in South Africa, Tonia grew up on an idyllic little farm above Van Reenen's Pass. As there was no suitable local school, she was sent to boarding school at the age of 5, a decision her parents later regretted.

Her secondary school years were transformative. From there she studied for a science degree at University of Natal, then taught secondary school mathematics for six years before opting for a year out. She spent over a year within the Arctic Circle in Tromso, Norway, getting to know her maternal grandmother's extensive family.

In 1973 Tonia moved to England where she joined the staff at Oxford University, working in research and teaching until 2001. Since then she has focused on her life-long love of writing and gardening. Her books span various categories: technical, self-help, biography and fiction as listed under
www.toniacopebowley.co.uk

Sadly, Tonia's husband, Stephen, passed in 2017. Her adult sons have nests of their own elsewhere. She lives in attractive rural Oxfordshire, UK, with her King Charles spaniel companions.

In 1988, Stephen and Tonia founded **The Thembisa Trust**, a charity that aims to give a chance in life to some of Southern Africa's most disadvantaged people. To learn more about Thembisa please go to:
www.thembisatrust.org

www.ingramcontent.com/pod-product-compliance
Lightning Source LLC
Chambersburg PA
CBHW070425010526
44118CB00014B/1908